Understanding Philp Larkin's Weddings" for A Level Stude

By Gavin Smithers

Another of **Gavin's Guides**- study books packed with insight. They aim to help you raise your grade!

Understanding Philip Larkin's "The Whitsun Weddings" for A Level Students is a complete study guide, written for students and teachers preparing for A level exams in 2018 and subsequent years.

This edition has been written to assist English Literature students and teachers with their coursework and final exams.

Series editor: Gill Chilton

Published by Gavin's Guides. All rights reserved. No part of this publication may be reproduced or transmitted in any form or by any means, electronic or mechanical, including photocopy, recording or any information storage and retrieval system, without the written prior permission of the publisher.   Copyright Gavin Smithers, 2018

The right of Gavin Smithers to be identified as the author of this work has been asserted in accordance with the Copyright, Designs and Patents Act 1988. This book is copyright material and must not be copied, reproduced, transferred, distributed, leased, licensed or publicly performed or used in any way except as specifically permitted in writing by the publishers, as allowed under the terms and conditions under which it was purchased or as strictly permitted by applicable copyright law. Any unauthorized distribution or use of this text may be a direct infringement of the author's and publisher's rights and those responsible may be liable in law accordingly.

You will need a copy of the poems:

"The Whitsun Weddings" by Philip Larkin is published by Faber & Faber. Available on Amazon.

Contents

Preface 4

Overview.. 8

Here 13

Mr Bleaney 17

Nothing to be Said 21

Love Songs in Age.. 23

Naturally the Foundation will bear your Expenses .26

Broadcast 28

Faith Healing 32

For Sidney Bechet 35

Home is so Sad 39

Toads Revisited 42

Water 45

The Whitsun Weddings 48

Self's the Man 53

Take one Home for the Kiddies 56

Days 58

MCMXIV 61

Talking in Bed 64

The Large Cool Store 66

A Study of Reading Habits 69

Contents

As Bad as a Mile 72

Ambulances 74

The Importance of Elsewhere 77

Sunny Prestatyn 78

First Sight 82

Dockery and Son 84

Ignorance 88

Reference Back 91

Wild Oats 94

Essential Beauty 99

Send No Money 101

Afternoons 104

An Arundel Tomb 107

Appendix 1:

Larkin's themes, methods and interests 111

Appendix 2: The Essays

Sample Essay 1 115

Sample Essay 2 118

Appendix 3: Key dates in Larkin's Life ....I......... 120

Appendix 4:

Dates of poems & social history context 122

Preface

Philip Larkin (1922-1985) is a significant figure in post- 1900 English and British poetry. At present, the WJEC exam board offers students Larkin's collection "The Whitsun Weddings" as one half of one of the five paired options for unit 2. The AS/A level qualification requires candidates to analyse one poem in detail, and to write an essay comparing Larkin and the counterpart poetry collection (at present, Carol Ann Duffy's "Mean Time").

You will find two sample essays, analysing different Larkin poems, at the end of this guide. The overall aim of my guide is to arm you with a sound analysis of each and every poem in "The Whitsun Weddings". Starting with my analysis, you can then build your own. My advice is that you must consider the form and structure of the poems; the persona of the narrator; the tone; the language of the poem; and any relevant context. This study guide will give you some stepping stones to ford that river.

The critical analysis requires evidence of your ability to explain how meaning is constructed, and the contribution to it of structure, form and language. Moreover, the cultural context of the poems should be considered- as it affects both the writer and the reader. This leads to an assessment and explanation of the values and attitudes which inform or motivate the poems, and how they have been and continue to be read.

This guide therefore includes an analytical commentary on each of the 32 poems which comprise "The Whitsun Weddings", and it explores connections between them. This leads us to appendices addressing Larkin's methods, his themes and interests, and the salient facts from his biography.

The only critical analyses of the poems I have seen do not consider their sequencing. The fact that there are thirty-two poems means that there is a very large range of options, as Larkin assembles them in the sequence he prefers. We should expect to find that the sequencing clarifies key themes; and that, just as a symphony will have three or four movements (or more), and differences in mood and tone, a collection or cycle of poems will work in a similar dimension. I suggest that, towards the end of the sequence, the tone becomes darker and more serious. The collection starts its journey by explaining why the poetic or narrative voice needs to maintain a distance or detachment between itself and its subject matter and scenery. Towards the end of the collection, the poems are much more close-up; they confront the ends of things, including the end of our own life (and its legacy, if any), directly. Despite the appeal- for some readers, and even his mistress Maeve Brennan- of sentimentalising the final couplet of the closing poem, Larkin is clear-sighted in his final view that, if anything is true, it is that death is extinction.

The first explicit death is in poem 14 ("Take One Home for the Kiddies") – of a pet. Then we have the following dead characters- Dockery and Cartwright (poem 24), dying smokers ("Essential Beauty", poem 29) and the Earl and Countess ("An Arundel Tomb", poem 32). There is a narrator whose own romance has died ("Wild Oats", poem 28), and one who cannot talk openly in bed (poem 16); there are the less seriously ill ambulatory patients in "Toads Revisited" (poem 10), and the dying ambulance patient in "Ambulances" (poem 20). The emotionally damaged, unloved women in "Faith Healing" (poem 7) give way to the victims of fantasy violence in poem 18, "A Study of Reading Habits", and then the more disturbing degrading of the poster girl in "Sunny Prestatyn", poem 22. After the recurrent idea that living is just slow dying, we have, in the closing poem, the Arundel Tomb, which is presented to us as the actual tomb of the 14th century lovers, now dying/dead for six centuries (although they are buried in Lewes Priory). The immobility of death is the final thought.

The collection is populated with characters who die; with dreams which die; with false assumptions about life and death, which should be killed off. But a certain dignity and resilience remains. That is why it would be wrong to call this collection "nihilistic" or hopeless. Larkin would present it as a clear-eyed, pragmatic view of what it means to be alive in post-war England.

Although I have written this guide with the requirements of the A-level assessment objectives in mind, I hope it will be useful for the general reader too; and for teachers, who will want to present a range of interpretations for their students to discuss.

My aim is that readers of this guide will be able to see the value of examining the form and structure of a poem as a clue to detecting its meaning. I have also scrutinised the language closely, because this is the most reliable interpretative method. Beware the vague (and lazy) substituting of what sometimes masquerades as analysis, but is really only an unexamined personal response. We need to be aware not only of how a poem changes us, but of how that comes about. With Larkin, it is a matter of tone and language.

Larkin's poems are often informed by specific places, familiar to him, and interactions he had with particular people. Where this is relevant or useful, I mention it. It does not mean that the narrators of the poems are Larkin; they are too different for that to be possible. It is more accurate to say that the speakers of these poems tend to have some experience in common with Larkin, and that he uses the vehicle of the poem to examine and universalise some of his own preoccupations (what is truth/ what is the meaning of being alive/ what are the pros and cons of human commitment and intimacy/how much are we prisoners of our accidentally formed habits and preferences?).

If you fall under Larkin's rather idiosyncratic spell, and you want to find out more about his life, I recommend Richard Bradford's "First Boredom, then Fear- the life of Philip Larkin", published by Peter Owen.

"The Whitsun Weddings" – Overview

Philip Larkin (1922- 1985) was never a full-time poet; after graduating from Oxford University with a first-class degree in English, he worked as a librarian, with some eventual distinction. The demands of his professional career often suppressed or delayed his writing of poems, but his poetry brought him a degree of public recognition which he welcomed and considered his due.

Larkin published three main collections of poems; "The Less Deceived" in 1955 (a collection derived from his time in Belfast); "The Whitsun Weddings" in 1964, by which time he had spent a decade as the librarian in charge at the University of Hull; and "High Windows", in 1974. He was never prolific, but in the last years of his life he wrote less and less.

The 1955 collection includes some very accomplished and interesting poems, and it is worth reading if you want to extend your understanding of Larkin's themes, his methods and his interests. Moreover, the poem "Toads Revisited" in "The Whitsun Weddings" refers back to the poem "Toads" in "The Less Deceived".

Reading the 1955 collection as well as- or, preferably, before - "The Whitsun Weddings" will help you to clarify aspects of Larkin's thought and outlook which become sharper and clearer as he becomes older. I think that we can capture the essence of what he is interested in partly by looking at the shared evidence in both collections.

The 1964 collection- 32 poems in all- is written with a strong sense of the shadow of our eventual death. It observes deaths past, present and future, and it argues that death will simply mark the end of our time; we all have a life which we can live or waste as we choose, and it does not really matter very much how we use it.

This may strike us as a macabre attitude, in a 42-year-old (especially when we discover that many of the poems were written several years earlier, when he was still in his 30s), but Larkin had lived through the Second World War (as a civilian, not a combatant) and his generation knew how cheap life can be and how fragile it is. He accepts the vulnerability of the human being, and the futility of all human life, with a clear gaze, and a consistent absence of self-pity and fuss.

Larkin makes poems out of everyday observations. He has a hunger for something he calls "truth", but his experience of seeking it is frustrating, because truth is relative. There are no keys which can unlock the door to meaning in our lives. This is the existentialist puzzle which occupied so many philosophers in the 1950s.

The poems contain a long and lively cast list of characters. Larkin is anti-consumerism; he sees advertising billboards as selling a lie ("Essential Beauty", "Sunny Prestatyn"). He is anti-religion, as he sees organised religion as hokum ("Water"), and a poor substitute for experiencing any form of deep love in your human relationships ("Faith Healing"). He does not patronise his characters. They may be middle-class, or working class; more, or less, educated; he is more interested in what unites us- the predicament all human lives are in- than what divides us. And what unites us is the inevitable reality that death will cut us off, which renders the question of the quality of our lives and our achievements (or lack of them) of little or no importance, except perhaps to ourselves.

A recurring theme in the collection is the elusiveness of what is true or real- the "distance" between our everyday experience and any universal or sustained understanding, and the elusiveness of any lasting satisfaction beyond the occasional "ecstasies". The search for meaning in our lives goes on, he says, until we die.

Whether you are Mr Bleaney, or a young mother from a housing estate in Hull, or the self-confident Oxford graduate Dockery, or Larkin himself, you face the same challenges of "boredom. Then fear". The human condition, as he perceives it, is essentially isolated, and we need our own emotional space. It is more tolerable when we- or the truth-seekers amongst us- cultivate a sense of emotional detachment, silence and, as the opening poem, "Here", observes, the "loneliness" of "removed lives".

As a poet, he himself has a heightened sense of detachment, but we are all (including Arnold in "Self's The Man") in danger of being pushed to the margins of our own lives ("Afternoons"), by a sense of the meaningless of our existence, and by the social demands of our close relatives and other people we meet.

Just as he had done in "The Less Deceived", Larkin includes some overtly autobiographical poems, as well as several where the identity of the narrator is not explicit. Somewhat autobiographical are "Mr Bleaney", "The Whitsun Weddings", "Self's the Man", "Dockery and Son", "Toads Revisited", "Send No Money" - poems where Larkin's narrator is recognisably Larkin, but the poem does not depend on this for its meaning.

More thoroughly autobiographical, perhaps, and therefore more intensely subjective in their reactions, are another group - "Naturally the Foundation.....", "Broadcast", "The Importance of Elsewhere", "For Sidney Bechet", "A Study of Reading Habits", "Wild Oats", "Home" and "Reference Back". These poems tend to deploy aspects of Larkin's autobiography and his tastes, without stepping outside of the experience to the same degree. These poems are much more focused on himself and much less on other people.

A third category is a selection of the poems which are informed by his own drives, including the nature of erotic stimulation, and hypochondria- "Sunny Prestatyn", "Ambulances" and "The Large Cool Store" are straightforward examples.

Then there is a group which takes a landscape or a scene or an object and draws out some significance from it (a metaphysical approach)- "Here",

"MCMXIV", "Afternoons", "An Arundel Tomb". Larkin preferred animals to children, and in "The Less Deceived" also, he uses animals as the embodiment of a non-human but valid experience- often, of vulnerability.

Finally, there are some philosophical or reflective poems- usually short ones- which use the animal world or anthropology to make an existential point- "Nothing to be Said", "Home is so Sad", "Water", "Take One Home for the Kiddies", "Days", "Talking in Bed", "As Bad as a Mile", "Ignorance".

While the individual poems are always succinct, and sometimes extremely short, there is a breadth and range of themes which guarantees that they are never dull to read, even if the lives they draw on can be dull. They belong together because they continue the journey from 1955, seeking insight in middle age into how we can achieve contentment, if we are pragmatists rather than fantasists about our own lives.

Try to identify groupings of your own, which fit clusters of the poems. Mine are not prescriptive, and whenever we return to the poems our groupings may change. The fact that there is no definitive way of grouping them does not matter; the value lies in its stimulus to us in identifying recurring themes and motifs, because these are the poet's subconscious fingerprints.

The sequence in which the poems are arranged is, however, specific. Our journey through the collection, as readers, invites us to connect poems, as if they are all running on some giant railway network. Your reading of them will be enriched if you attune yourself to the language and tone of the poems- you will see which ones are following the same track.

Here is my analysis of each poem, in their sequence.

Here

The collection contains 32 poems, and this opening poem has 32 lines (four octets). It begins with three repetitions of the word "swerving" and it ends with three of the word "here"- in addition to its use as the title for the poem. The title of the poem refers to Hull and its surroundings. Larkin had moved there in 1955, from Belfast, to take up his appointment as the University Librarian.

Stanzas 1 and 3 have an identical rhyme scheme (ABABCDDC), and so do stanzas 2 and 4 (ABBACDDC), which helps to unify the poem; the lengths of lines vary between 9 and 11 syllables, with the average line length shortening towards the end of the poem, as it gathers pace.

The two central stanzas zoom in on details of Hull itself, while the outer stanzas give its geographical surroundings- farmland to the south, and the North Sea to the east in stanza 4.

Key words are solitude (line 5), pastoral (line 20), isolate and removed (line 24), loneliness and silence (25), unnoticed (line 26), hidden (27), distance (28), existence (23), untalkative and out of reach (24). The poet-narrator sees the town as uninteresting- its architectural variety is listed without engagement or comment- and populated by trolley-stealers, "grim head-scarfed wives" and salesmen.

The consumer objects are "desires", and they are listed like television game show prizes. The narrator's desire is not to acquire cheap or cut-price bargains, but to maintain his silence and keep his distance- in other words, the collection of poems which follow will be detached and objective in its observation of people's way of life.

The word "pastoral" suggests not only that the narrator's interests lie in the rural hinterland, which is less populated and more colourful than the still-developing urban environment, but that the unfinished town of Hull (with its cranes and its "dead", straight roads from the outlying new build houses to the shops) is grotesque. "Fishy-smelling" has a literal meaning (as a fishing port, Hull does smell of fish) but the inference is also that it smells odd or suspicious, with its strange mixture of consulates, department stores, the slave museum (William Wilberforce, who led the abolition of the slave trade, was born here) and the tattoo-shops, and the very surprising image of "ships up streets" (the fishing boats are moored and visible from some of the shopping areas in the centre of Hull).

Stanza 1 brings us (by train) into the railway station and the town centre; the train journey out of Hull resumes in line 22, and the narrator embraces the sense of growing obscurity and isolation as the journey goes all the way to the North Sea. Where the sea meets the end of the beach, the sun is up and the temperature is warm- there is no need for head-scarves (whereas, in reality, if you need one in Hull you will also need it at the coast). The only two similes- an elevated, poetic device- are reserved for the pleasure of isolation (lines 23, 26).

The punctuation is notable, in that the opening sentence takes twenty-four and a half lines. Then, in the final stanza, there is room for three more sentences, each of them starting with "here".

The language has some distinctive characteristics. Larkin uses adjectives and nouns in pairs (thin and thistled, skies and scarecrows etc). Quite often these pairings are alliterative, but there are other instances of alliteration too (night north, harsh-named halt, swerving to solitude etc).

If you analyse the adjectives, you will see that he often uses more than one (rich industrial, thin and thistle, piled gold, shining gull-marked, dead straight, grim head-scarfed, mortgaged half-built, bluish neutral) and that many of them are double-barrelled, compounds (harsh-named, grain-scattered etc). The compounding extends to some nouns too (kitchen-ware, tattoo-shops, wheat-fields).

This would seem self-indulgent, but it is offset by the extensive use of monosyllables, which account for 58% of all the words in the poem.

Perhaps this antithesis between the simple and the more complex and elusive (which requires a forensic precision in the use of language to capture it) symbolises the distinction between the narrator's complex relationship with the pastoral, the beach and the fields and hedges, which are isolated/unfenced/out of reach- a place of freedom, and his more straightforward detachment from the urban; or the distinctions between the half-built and the unbuilt, the old and the new.

The lexical field of death and burial grounds impinges on the poem (shadows/ statues/ spires/ brought down/ dead/ terminate/ grim/ removed lives/ silence/ unnoticed/weeds/ neglected/ ends/ out of reach). What you lose in Hull is also your individuality- people exist in categories (workmen, residents, salesmen, relations, wives), not as individuals who can be distinguished from one another.

The first three stanzas are quite easy to read aloud; they use an iambic pentameter metre in a comprehensible way. The final stanza does something different; it is like an untangling of something tightly wound. "Loneliness clarifies" in line 25 really belongs before "removed lives", and "leaves thicken unnoticed" would be easier in line 26, though it would spoil the rhyme. The verb "ends" is brought forward in line 30 ("the land suddenly ends/ ends suddenly" would be more straightforward). Torturing the syntax is suggestive of the pain involved in reaching the nirvana of "unfenced existence" and the counter-intuitive idea that human beings, who congregate in towns and cities, really need to be alone and "out of reach". At the end of line 31, the metre highlights the word "existence", because the first and third syllables are stressed; when we speak the word, the stressed syllable is the middle one.

Changing the stress relates the noun to the adjective, so that the poem becomes "existential"- a clue that the collection as a whole will address the central preoccupation of what our lives are for.

"Loneliness clarifies" becomes an epigram, because it is placed at the start of the final stanza. We tend to deprecate loneliness, but the narrative persona here is reassuring us that it serves to help us understand what we would otherwise fail to; the poet's condition of solitude, isolation, loneliness lends "distance" or perspective. Thus, because of his loneliness, we, the readers of the poems, do not have to take on the same discomfort in order to garner the same insights or perspectives.

Mr Bleaney

Mr Bleaney- and the narrator, who follows him as a kind of ghost in the making- is a man who has a name but still manages to be anonymous. Larkin himself so disliked owning bricks and mortar that he always rented his accommodation until the advanced age of 51.

The poem is in seven quatrains with a rhyme scheme ABAB. Its extreme regularity and predictability reenact those characteristics of Bleaney's life, and the narrator's.

Lines 1-9 are a dialogue between the narrator and his prospective landlady. The mock- heroic, impulsive decision "I'll take it" (line 10) then puts the narrator in the shoes of his predecessor- except that Bleaney's encouragement led to extra (deafening) noise, from a TV set or a radio. The final two stanzas contain the narrator's reflections- ostensibly about Bleaney, but ironically, as the reader will recognise, about his own life and lack of achievement. In later poems, Dockery and Arnold will serve a similar purpose.

The drab details of Bleaney's routine emerge alongside the drab details of the furnished room, with its ill-fitting, terrible curtains, its depressing view, the absence of a comfortable chair, a lightshade, an ash-tray; its "fusty" bed and inadequate heating. The landlady says that he had stayed until his employer (the Bodies) relocated him, but the phrase "they moved him", together with his employers' name, makes us shiver a little too, because it is redolent of being removed by an undertaker. Indeed, the room is so sparse that it could almost be a funeral parlour, or a prison cell. There has for many years been a funeral director in Hull called "Boddy's"- its current incarnation is as TS Annison and R Boddy Funeral Directors.

The sense of comic pathos is heightened by Bleaney's habitual "plugging at the four aways"- the football pools, where the almost impossible (but cheap) bet on four teams to win away from home would net a useful return. A man with no apparent social or sex life had clung to a small dream of being able to escape to a different sort of life, but it was a futile piece of resistance- he did not move because he won a fortune.

Although it is subliminal, the lexis of death, or the fear of death, haunts the poem- the Bodies/they moved him/ flowered curtains/ thin and frayed/ lie/lay/ frigid/ dread/ one hired box (a coffin). Bleaney's life is a dramatisation of the idea in "Dockery and Son" that a human life is a process of "first boredom, then fear", and then death.

In contrast with "Here", there are very few adjectives in this poem- because there is so little to describe. The description is done by elimination – no hook, no room- and we could add to this list all the other things Bleaney lacked- no friends, no warmth, no sex, no love, no prospects, no success, no hope................

The technique in the final two stanzas is similar to that in "Here"; a complex sentence with idiosyncratic syntax ends with the key, concluding words ("I don't know" for "out of reach"). The narrator's attempt to think what Bleaney thought peters out, as if the effort to find something to be positive about is too great to manage. The bon mot "how we live measures our own nature" exposes the bareness of Bleaney's life, as well as his room, and the sentence is a rather cruel judgment- he should surely have realised that he had no real prospect of changing his life or raising his horizons. Bleaney's future is as bleak as his past- supposing that he is still alive and has had a job move.

The potential nihilism of this judgment is softened, for the reader, by the irony that the narrator is becoming Bleaney, by living just as he did; his existence is conducted on equally cramped terms, without physical possessions or emotional attachments. The final line makes the point that such a life has no point; why anyone would accept it, or settle for it, is unfathomable. But Bleaney, like so many of the narrators and characters in these poems, lacks personal ambition and drive.

The rhetorical peroration which starts at line 26 is reminiscent of Wilfred Owen's "Dulce et Decorum Est" ("if you could hear……you would not") but Larkin makes his exhortation bathetic instead, because Owen's moral outrage would be inappropriate here- Mr Bleaney has been wasting his life voluntarily, and has not been deceived by anyone.

There is something of Owen, too, in the alliteration in the poem- specifically, the use of nine words starting with "f". Owen uses alliteration to convey disgust at the sense of human life being wasted, and to expose complacency; the same thing is happening here, in a less overt and obvious way.

The final words -"I don't know"- turn the glaring light of the sixty-watt bulb back on to the narrator. His lack of self-confidence, his own ineffectual muddle of a life, makes Bleaney's existential problem the narrator's too.

Nothing To Be Said

If the previous poem was designed to close the gap between us and its protagonist- to leave us asking ourselves how much of Bleaney's drift and obscurity infects us, and whether that is tolerable or not- the third poem in the collection reminds us that death is the universal condition of being alive, and that, when we see our lives in that light, what we do in them has no lasting significance anyway.

The poem, in three sestets, relies on repetition and what appears at first to be antithesis to make its points. It compares a primitive society with a so-called developed or advanced one, beginning with the unevolved, irascible, short, outdoor, Neolithic hunter-gatherers. Modern society is organised in families, rather than tribes, and its stones are cobblestones in mill-towns (in Lancashire or Yorkshire, after the Industrial Revolution); they now hold garden parties and give evidence in court.

The middle stanza makes the distinction between modes or methods of doing things, but the ancients and the moderns are both preoccupied with the same things- building, measuring love and money, and benediction (one might say, rather like the institution of the Church; perhaps the unexpected choice of "cross-faced" is intended to accentuate the reader's awareness that organised religion is a construct to help us avoid the blank, bleak truth about death).

Lines 6, 10 and 13 focus on the similarities which unite humanity over long stretches of time, and the evolution of consumerism, using the words slow/slowly and dying/death to support the oxymoronic assertion in line 6; and then the repetition of "nothing" in the final two lines gives them a neat double meaning.

Civilisations die out and leave nothing behind them, no evidence of their lives; and recognising that living is merely an extended process of dying is unanswerable and unchallengeable- inescapable- so that "it leaves/ Nothing to be said".

Incidentally, this combination of slow dying and "nothing" is reminiscent of another Wilfred Owen poem- "Exposure". Larkin uses it again in "Dockery and Son".

Love Songs in Age

This poem is in three octets; it concerns the paper music of three songs, which are enumerated in the opening stanza. In the final stanza, there is another trinity- "solve....satisfy....set in order".

The rhyme scheme is identical in stanzas one and two- ABABBBCC- but there is an ever so subtle shift in stanza three, regarding the placing of the key verb, "satisfy". A poem in which the failure of the sentiments in love songs to do what they promise to do- at least from the perspective of age and widowhood- displaces the word "satisfy" from its expected position, nudges it aside; if the rhymes were to follow the pattern of the preceding stanzas, we would expect the rhymes to be love/show/above/so/satisfy/cry/how/now. The swapping of "satisfy" and "so" is unsatisfactory, just as the promises the love songs contained "had not" been fulfilled in the youth of the subject of the poem, and "could not now".

As we saw with "Here", Larkin uses a long opening sentence- here it occupies all but the last three words of stanza 2, and takes 106 words- to give the reader a set of detailed images; in this case, the three pieces of sheet music, and, particularly, the marks on them. "Her songs" is ambiguous; we know that she used to play them (line 16); did she in fact compose them? If so, their failure to "solve.....and set....in order" would be more poignant because it would be more personal.

Stanza 1 makes it clear that the reason "she kept her songs" was because of their emotional associations, but not specifically to do with her marriage. Stanza 2 starts with an image of the sheet music, with the chordal introductions and the lyrics hyphenated across the bars of the music; the emotional association is with the "unfailing sense" and "certainty" that a long life lies before you. One of only two "sprawling hyphenated word"(s) in the poem is "spring-woken" in line 13, which is attached, in the only simile, to the symbol of the tree- not an elderly or dying tree, but one with "freshness". When she played these songs (on the piano), the songs gave her a perception of the almost magical quality of love.

This characterisation of love and of the tree expresses an emotional need for stability- not the boredom we find elsewhere in some of the poems, but the sense of being empowered by marriage which we find in the last lines of "The Whitsun Weddings". There, as here, that power turns to "a sense of falling", as the natural state of being alone (as in widowhood) becomes customary. In "The Whitsun Weddings" , "Self's the Man" and "The Large Cool Store", love and marriage are presented as temporary or fleeting "ecstasies" which flatten into a longer experience, or perspective, of disappointment and regret (and so should be avoided).

In "Faith Healing", the supplicants are "the women" – not men- and they go to the healer because they want to get a sense of "all they might have done had they been loved".

Because the words of the three songs have not changed, they still hold out the false promise that love (in its abstract, not yet experienced conception, for the young) can and will be the solution to everything. The conclusion of the poem is that that was always a false premise, and it will always remain so.

Music/song features in several of the poems in this group ("Broadcast", "For Sidney Bechet", "Reference Back") but only here is it labelled as meretricious or deceiving. "Reference Back" is another poem about emotional associations across time; the poet-narrator plays a record made in 1923, thirty years later, and the memory of discovering or hearing it originally has the effect of making the intervening decades seem to be a process of diminishment or diminution- horizons darken and narrow, and we become conscious of "our losses", as though life is a process of gradually parting with what made it seem rich when we were young. This includes the death of parents and the ending of romantic relationships.

The language in "Love Songs in Age" is relatively inert. Just as "songs" begins with an "s", there are 21 words beginning with an "s" sound in the poem (out of a total of 159). Stanza 1 is full of passive verbs, and, even when she (accidentally) finds the songs, the protagonist stands, like a statue; there is no movement.

Adjectives are infrequent- there are only fourteen, mainly clustered in the central stanza, where the memories break out. Just as Mr Bleaney had accepted the constraints of a life without any emotional intensity (an approach Larkin endorses in his earlier poem, "Reasons for Attendance", though his reasons are different), so the elderly widow here has no capacity to find "That brilliance, love", because its brilliance is an illusion.

Naturally the Foundation will Bear Your Expenses

This is another poem in three octets with an ABABCDCD rhyme scheme. The narrator is probably an academic (a fellow Professor of Professor Lal) and an egomaniac; his ego seems almost bigger than England itself, and the pronouns I, me and my feature ten times altogether. He could, alternatively, be a pastiche of a self-important literary figure (Chatto was a publisher of serious literary fiction, and E M Forster was an eminent novelist, most famous for his 1924 novel "A Passage to India"- the same journey the narrator is going to make).

The poem Is a dramatic monologue, and the accidental, self-condemning revelations focus on the narrator's attitude to Remembrance Day. He is utterly unemotional, and he dismisses the Remembrance ceremony as "mawkish" and England as infantile. The external world is an intrusive nuisance. He clucks alliteratively at the "crowds, colourless and careworn" and dismissively at the "wreath-rubbish" with its "solemn-sinister" character. He is acquisitive (your expenses/ snatch...the sunshine) and possessive (my Comet/ my taxi/ my contact and my pal).

Because Larkin himself benefited from having his poetry publicised on the Third programme (the forerunner of BBC Radio 3, but a speech and music channel in the early 1960s, which some people thought too academic and high-brow), some readers infer that the narrator here is Larkin himself. This seems unlikely, partly because he was an infrequent international traveller.

The de Haviland Comet first went into service in the early 1950s; as a jet plane it was as innovative as Concorde would be later, but it suffered serious safety problems, with a number of fatal accidents in the early 1960s, even after its design had been modified. Readers who are especially struck by this narrator's lack of empathy and gratitude to others may feel that, if he were involved in such a fatal crash, it would not be such a tragedy!

Throughout the poem, there is intra-line alliteration; this reinforces the sense of the narrator's insufferable self-satisfaction. His refusal to acknowledge other people as important or legitimate extends to his abbreviation of (the) Queen and (the Prime) Minister, and he is so self-absorbed as to be unaware of one of the most important anniversaries in his national history.

Larkin's preference is to take details of his own daily life and work them into poems with a thoughtful, wry, speculative tone, and a sophisticated degree of self-awareness; the voice is rarely as unpleasant as this one is. Perhaps he felt that the poems in "The Less Deceived" had been too personal in character, and that he needed, now, to invent a wider range of voices and registers. The nearest comparison in the 1964 collection is "A Study of Reading Habits", which contains more recognisably autobiographical material, but edges into aggression and a misogynistic violence which sits on the edge of being grotesque.

Broadcast

This poem is in three sestets, with a rhyme scheme ABACCB. Its origin lies in a concert at Hull City Hall on 5/11/1961 and its addressee is Maeve Brennan. She was at the concert, which Larkin could hear on the radio; the repertoire was Elgar (Larkin would choose Elgar's First Symphony as one of his "Desert Island Discs"). Maeve was a member of staff at the Hull University Library, whom Larkin had helped to prepare for vocational exams. She had graduated at Hull University in 1951 and worked at the Hull City Library, where she set up a music library, before moving to the University Library in 1953; Larkin would arrive there two years later.

Larkin had a longstanding relationship, from 1950, until his death in 1984, with Monica Jones (1922-2001) (although they saw each other quite infrequently; she worked in Leicester, 100 miles away by car- although Larkin habitually travelled by train). Maeve (1929-2003) was a staunch Roman Catholic and therefore sexually unavailable to him, at least until 1963, according to his own explanation of the reference to that year in his poem "Annus Mirabilis"- although that line is explicable in other terms, too, regarding the Profumo affair and the lifting of the obscenity ban on DH Lawrence's "Lady Chatterley's Lover".

It may have suited Larkin that marriage, as a condition for taking his relationship with Maeve further, was a commitment too far for him (on the grounds of religious incompatibility), so that he did not have to make a decisive break with Monica. In 1961, he had to justify or excuse his interest in Maeve to Monica, whom he had almost offered to marry in 1955, in terms similar to the thesis of "Self's the Man"- "I don't want to lose you"- while expressing less than total sureness about the idea.

Through a remarkable frankness and lack of sensitivity, Larkin managed to maintain a kind of menage a trois until the late 1970s with both women alternately. Monica was his intellectual equal but Maeve appealed to his disrespect for religion, and she was a work colleague and therefore ever-present.

In "Wild Oats", Larkin reveals that a pretty female face sends him into raptures; he also seems to have found erotic interest in Monica's choice of clothing, and in Maeve's shoes. In "Broadcast", there are undertones of the erotic or of fetishism, which the poet-narrator wisely transfers to the orchestra and the audience in the hall- "cascades of monumental slithering/ leaving me desperate"; this is an extension of the "ecstasies" he imagines can be inspired by the feminine nightwear available in "The Large Cool Store". The discarded glove, next to the fetishized shoes, implies a striptease, but nothing so direct is said; instead, Maeve is complimented for being "beautiful and devout". Her religious devotion intensifies his longing for her, because it appears to accentuate her unavailability. The first four lines of the poem are a sort of introductory foreplay, before the narrator's attention settles on her. He enjoys the thought of her more in the dark.

We know from "Here" that "distance" (emotional detachment) is important in giving the poet perspective and insight. In "Talking in Bed", the physical proximity to another person is stressful because it is a (too short) "unique distance from isolation". In "Ambulances", the stricken patient is being driven away from his family and from his own life and identity. Distance is creatively and emotionally stimulating for Larkin- otherwise his long-distance relationship with Monica would not have endured- so that, although the physical distance from his flat to the concert hall is only 1.7 miles, the absence of visual cues where he sits renders him "shamelessly.....desperate".

"Talking in Bed" implies that the poet-narrator would feel inhibited from expressing his devotion- or, more precisely, its intensity and the cues which prompt it (face, gloves, shoes)- if the addressee were with him, listening to the broadcast. Her absence intensifies her overpowering attraction. With typical, inseparable ambivalence on Larkin's part, we can see that the poem, while ostensibly aimed at Maeve, is also an effective commentary on his feelings for Monica.

A closer look at the language is interesting. The City Hall is exaggerated in its size- giant/ vast/ huge/ monumental- while the addressee of the poem is "tiny", her glove "unnoticed". The audience makes various noises before and after the National Anthem is played, as a prelude to the concert, but some of the actions ascribed to it also describe sexual activity which the participants in it may want to do in the dark, and keep unseen- whispering/ slithering etc.

The addressee, though tiny, has the capacity to "overpower" the narrator, although hers is one face amidst "all those faces", and this anonymity and apparent insignificance serves to intensify the gravitational pull she exerts on him. The conjunction of tiny and hands is a musical reference to the aria in Puccini's "La Boheme" "Che gelida manina"- your tiny hand is frozen; the "wavebands" which transmit the music are glowing, but the object of the narrator's adoration is "leaving me desperate" by being "frigid" (to borrow the description of the wind in "Mr Bleaney").

In "La Boheme", two lovers, Rodolfo (a poet) and Mimi (a seamstress), live in an attic (like Larkin's small second-storey apartment at 32 Pearson Park), where they fall in love, in the dark. Mimi develops a cough and is dying from tuberculosis; they separate amicably, but some months later she returns, and dies in the flat.

Larkin had used the same technique- listening to the same broadcast, or reading the same book, and discussing it later- to create a shared closeness with Monica which compensated for the physical distance between them. Here he cannibalises that approach, to suggest to Maeve that she should fall in love with him, and that her tiny hands make her like Mimi, and him like Rodolfo- who is, coincidentally, also a poet.

On a more prosaic level, this poem neatly solves the issue felt so keenly in "Talking in Bed"- that emotional honesty in easier, at least for people like Larkin, when you are not in the same bed, or even the same building.

Faith Healing

This is the fifth consecutive three-stanza poem. It is written mostly in iambic pentameters, but lines 7, 16, 25 and 29 have 11 syllables. The rhyme scheme is identical in the first two stanzas- ABCABDABCD- but there is a subtle change in the third stanza, to ABCABCABCC.

Faith healing was popular in the USA from the 1950s to the 1980s, and it is closely associated with evangelical Christianity or Pentecostalism. One of its most famous practitioners was Oral Roberts (1918-

2009). The practice continues in the UK today, with ongoing debates about its effectiveness.

The structure of the poem is typical of what we have already seen in other poems- an exposition of the scene in stanza 1; a mixture of description and analysis in stanza 2; and a concluding, if sometimes tentative, principle, extracted in the concluding third stanza.

This is not an overtly anti-religious poem (God is mentioned only once, in passing, in line 9), because its focus is on the emotional needs, specifically, of women (line 1), to whom a patriarchal, charismatic figure seems to appeal. This relates to the use of "submissive" in line 9 of "Love Songs in Age" and the comments on women in general in the final stanza of "The Large Cool Store", claiming that women are "unearthly" and emotionally different from men. They are attracted by the demonstrative "warm spring rain of loving care" of the laying on of hands; it evokes joy in them, and an ecstatic (orgasmic?) "twitching" or "shake", succeeded by "an immense slackening ache".

The third stanza puts forward a theory about emotional need; everyone, the narrator observes, responds to it either by "loving others" (in the Christian sense of doing good), or by way of a sense of what might have been possible for them, together with a sense of deprivation, of unrealised potential, of disempowerment, which could just possibly be cured or healed if they came to feel that they were the recipient or object of more "loving care".

The process described in lines 6-11 is notable for its assembly-line speed and consistency; the healing process is impersonal and is allocated "some twenty seconds". That is enough to provoke a physical reaction, but, to borrow again from "The Large Cool Store", this is "synthetic, new/ and natureless". This response, while ecstatic, is misguided, because the "ache" to experience being loved is incurable and deep. The women are thus defined as unintelligent or "thick"- their tongues stand for them.

The word "blort" in line 19 is itself synthetic- a perhaps tearful, and certainly incoherent, combination of "blow" and "snort".

The similes further reinforce the sense that thinking the faith healer can cure the underlying malady is naïve. The unthinking tears of joy at the perception of a momentary kindness is what you would expect from "a kind of dumb/ And idiot child". The women, having had their twenty seconds, are sent away "like losing thoughts". Loss and losing is a metaphor in Larkin's poems for the process of decay/decline (the closing lines of "Maiden Name", stanza 4 of "Ambulances", stanza 3 of "Reference Back"). The brief intervention of a perceived kindness does not and cannot arrest the deeper decline which leads to the disappointment of "Love Songs in Age".

The final stanza answers the faith healer's question in line 7. What's wrong is not a physical ailment but the damage to your psyche that a perceived and felt lack of love generates. Twenty seconds of someone's attention is not enough to nurture a lasting sense of well-being.

The metre of the poem is uneasy. In lines 5, 13 and 19, there are clusters of stressed syllables, and a minimum of two or three lines in each stanza are a bad fit for the metre. This dislocation of the metre is beneath the surface, because the poem is partly concerned with the desire to follow the crowd, and hide one's distress; the underlying issue of what's wrong remains unsolved.

Larkin uses alliteration sparely here, and for two strategic reasons. Firstly, its infrequency adds bite to the blunt and unalert credulousness of the faith healing disciples (sheepishly stray/some stay stiff/ still survives etc). Secondly, it highlights the key aphorism that we all have a subconscious "sense of life lived according to love"- the gap between what we feel we are and what we (or these women) feel we could have been is what we have lost, but in fact we never had it- the sustained and sustaining loving care, joy and kindness which is always absent from the lives of the characters in Larkin's poems. The absence of it generates tears- there is water in lines 5, 14, 19 and 28.

For Sidney Bechet

As well as being a professional librarian, Larkin was a great jazz enthusiast and a correspondent on it for the Daily Telegraph for several years (1961-68).

Bechet (1897-1959) was a saxophonist and clarinettist who married late (1951) and was deported from England in 1922 (after attacking a woman) and from France in 1929 (after a gun fight). He was often accused of being self-centred and a misogynist; character traits which attach equally to some perceptions of Larkin.

This poem is rooted in New Orleans, Bechet's home town, where he began his career; Crescent City is a name for New Orleans, and Storyville is its red light district, where prostitution and drugs were licensed from 1897 until 1917.

The poem is in tercets, except for the couplet with which it ends. The rhyme scheme coheres in the first eight lines- ABABCDCD- and again in the last nine- EFEFEGEEG. Perhaps the fact that a balancing line is missing at the end of the poem- to make the couplet into another tercet- asserts the freedom of the musical form of jazz.

Once again, we find sentence lengths reducing as the poem approaches its conclusion. The exclamation in line 7 barely qualifies as a sentence-end; the first four tercets, or twelve lines, are voiced virtually all in one long saxophonist's breath. These lines address the evocative power of music, which is different for every individual listener. Here, the narrator observes that these perceptions are all "falsehoods" (ie not the truth) but "appropriate" ones. Some people may hear Bechet and think of a romanticised New Orleans (lines 4-6); some others, the escapism and anonymity of the alternative society of the brothel; but, for the poet-narrator, the music provokes less the imagination or a sense of a particular place, but more the affirmative ("an enormous yes"), like the emotion of love.

In the closing four lines, the narrator singles Bechet out for particular praise; in the narrator's version of New Orleans, there is no other music to be heard, because his has a unique power to dispel "long-haired grief and scored pity"- that is, pity which is an engraved, or deeply felt, sense of regret, and grief which is long-established, or perhaps grief attached to the loss of a woman with long hair?

For Larkin, jazz would induce a feeling of individual and personal warmth and comfort; he defined selfishness as "like listening to good jazz/ With drinks for further orders and a huge fire" (in the unpublished 1960 poem "None of the books have time").

The only word repeated in the poem is "love" (lines 6, 13). The jazz world allows you freedom (license), to lose yourself (manques) and escape (pretend) from the day-to-day world of "scholars".

The poem contrasts being in a "mute" environment, the brothel, where expensive girls will indulge your "fads", with the more authentic and joyful "natural noise" of the Bechet voice and speech - through music.

The narrator makes the distinction between the "appropriate falsehood" the listener to Bechet creates- feeling what is expressed in stanza 2- and the apparently inappropriate fantasies of the silent brothels. Both of these activities are temporary, transient diversions, but the poem is in no doubt that the music is both the cheaper and the more satisfying of the two. Larkin's marked enthusiasm for jazz was typical of his generation. The stimulation and emotional satisfaction music gave him seems analogous to what he sought in female company, and, from his point of view, it may have been more reliably found in music.

The suggestion that the prostitutes are "priced / far above rubies" invokes three texts from the Old Testament- "the price of wisdom is above rubies" (Nehemiah 28:18); "wisdom is better than rubies" (Proverbs 8:11); and "who can find a virtuous woman? For her price is far above rubies" (Ecclesiastes 31:10).

The three similes in the poem are lyrical about the other aspects of New Orleans (lines 2, 14) and unambiguous about the ferocity of the brothels (line 9); the poem prescribes jazz, not commercial sex, as the most effective pain relief for grief and (self-) pity.

Home is so Sad

Larkin completed this poem on a visit to his mother's house at Loughborough on New Year's Eve 1958.

Larkin's affinity with Thomas Hardy is well documented, and this elegiac short poem owes much to Hardy in terms of its form and organisation. The two stanzas, in iambic pentameters, rhyme ABABA ABABA. The long second sentence straddles the stanza break, and then gives way to two shorter ones. The final two-word sentence is like a tearful, gratuitous twist of the knife (of long-haired grief?). It ends the poem on a note of pure misery.

The house is personified, desolate, abandoned by the last of its occupants, who has stolen away, or been stolen away (by death) by "the theft". The house has no heart- which is literally true- but this means, too, that it has no energy or drive to maintain its own continuity, just as a bereaved person may have no inclination to go through the dull routine of daily life.

It is further personified, still in stanza 1, as "bereft of anyone to please", as if it were a domestic pet- possibly a pet dog. The departure of the last human occupant leaves it no purpose or focus.

The one slightly contemporary metaphor comes in lines 7-8- that of the house as a footballer, the goal (cleverly) as "how things ought to be". The house has taken a shot, which has missed, and it has no desire to resume its efforts with another shot, now that there is no-one living there.

The final lines address the reader directly, and force us to visualise four items of a domestic character; four things that make a house a home; the pictures, the cutlery, the music and "that vase".

Although these items will have a different meaning for the poet-narrator and the reader, we can still empathise vicariously because they have a universal or at least broad symbolism. Sheet music featured in "Love Songs in Age", and possibly in the "scored pity" which ends the previous poem, as that phrase may allude to musical scores or written notation (less fluid than Bechet's improvisatory playing by ear).

A good example of an equivalent poem by Hardy is "I look into my glass", in which the speaker sees his wasting skin in his mirror and wishes that his "heart had shrunk as thin"; he could then await his own death, "undistrest" and "with equanimity", because he would be undisturbed by emotional stimuli. However (cruel) Time will not let him shut off his residual desire for human contact, at night, and so "lets part abide" although it "part steals".

One reading of this is that the bereaved elderly person is wasting away through grief and loneliness, but while they experience what Larkin calls, in his poem "Wants", "the wish to be alone......desire of oblivion", they are not yet ready to die. Hardy uses the shrinking heart and the idea of theft (of the will to live) to convey his speaker's despair; Larkin recreates this as "having no heart", and the theft of dying which has stolen away the survivor who lived here (a widowed parent?).

Both poets personify an object (the organ of skin, a house) as something living, suffering, and grieving- Hardy chooses to describe it as "wasting", Larkin as "it withers"; in each case, natural growth and function has gone into reverse and will decline into extinction/death as a result of its paralysis by grief.

Larkin's imagery is more precise and concrete than it is in Hardy's poem; he resorts to telling us what the speaker's feelings are in his second stanza, while Larkin shows us. Larkin's use of the shift from the present to the past tense is effective ("You can see how it was"), as is the direct address to the reader; and his use of caesurae is alien to Hardy's treatment of a similar theme.

Both poems strike an elegiac note. Hardy's emotion is more bare and intense, but the symbolism of "noontide" and "eve" seems tired and trite. I suggest you do a comparative analysis of these two poems for yourself; regardless of which you prefer, it will give you a feeling for how Hardy influences Larkin.

Larkin's father Sydney had died in 1948; his mother lived from 1886 till November 1977. Larkin's own family situation, therefore, would not have generated the poem without an imaginative leap forward, thinking of the house as emptied of both his parents.

Toads Revisited

This poem is in 9 stanzas, comprising 36 lines in total. It uses an ABAB rhyme scheme, but some of the rhymes are tentative or weak.

The narrator appears to offer a thesis that work is good for us, framed in an urgent, persuasive, rhetorical speech. But it is a dramatic monologue and, as we look more closely at the narrator's assertion that various people who are too ill or old to work (lines 11-18) are shirkers; losers, with empty lives (lines 20-28), we find that his categorisation is wrong. His work is a crutch which he uses to help him navigate the emptiness of his own life.

The exclamation in line 19 is repeated and extended (without the exclamation mark); it is then explained, in lines 20-28. The problem, as he defines it, is that having no job reduces your life to a series of meaningless "failures" and makes it impossible for you to sustain friendships. What he is afraid of emerges in the rhetorical question in lines 32-34; darkness, solitude, and his own company.

This is interesting because, for Larkin, solitude was essential to creativity. The narrative persona he is presenting to us here is the opposite of this, and jittery himself- uncomfortable in his own skin. He is possessive about his in-tray and his secretary ("my" three times in lines 29-31). It is only the fact that he is needed in a work capacity, or the self-importance he attaches to himself, that separates him from the moribund shirkers he has described so unsympathetically in lines 11-16.

There is a lexical field of ill-health and hospitals in those descriptions- nurses/ out-patients/ accidents/ characters in long coats/ some bed- and, more broadly, with the in-tray/ secretary/ empty chairs/ cemetery. The association is so effective that, when we read about the long coats, we expect them to denote doctors or hospital consultants, and it is a surprise and a joke when we realise they are worn by tramps and vagrants.

If, like me, you find the most memorable item on the cast-list here the "hare-eyed clerks with the jitters", then the poem is juxtaposing the overtly diagnosed mentally ill and those who are on the verge of losing their psychological balance (like the narrator himself). He should be saying to himself "There but for the grace of God go I", not gloating over the ill-health of others and attributing it to their own weaknesses and failures.

The half-rhymes and the brisk metre of the poem help to form our perception of this narrator- smug, a thinker in black and white, an egotist, and someone who sees others' lives in negative terms (lines 7, 8, 27, 28, 29 all have a variant of "no" in them).

In "Faith Healing", the attending crowd was made up entirely of women. In this poem, apart from the nurses and the secretary, there are no women; all the patients are men. Perhaps, having examined the emotional fragility of the female psyche in "Faith Healing", "Toads Revisited" does the same with the psychology of the male, whose ego depends on validating himself as a stronger competitor in a tribe where the old and the palsied, the stupid or weak, are expendable, and lose their well-being when they forfeit their economic identity.

The impression of the narrator's own mania derives also from the punctuation; apart from the exclamation mark in line 19, up to the final couplet, the whole poem is a self-obsessed stream of consciousness, a querulous extended rhetorical question, in which the narrator misses the real, existential question, of how we ought to live or "be" (lines 7, 9, 18, 19, 24 all include be or being); of why human beings should extend some degree of sympathetic understanding to each other.

The repeated imperatives "give me" in lines 29 and 35 remind me of the imperatives "Bring me……." In Blake's "Jerusalem"; the narrator here sees the park as a green and potentially pleasant land, except for the shirkers who are in it.

The setting of the park and the office implies that the narrator's persona, while not Larkin, has grown out of his own self. We can see this in others of the poems, too- "Home is So Sad", where the narrator has probably lost both parents, and Larkin has not; and "A Study of Reading Habits", where the narrator is a kind of mini-Larkin with the aggression of a Rottweiler or a Dracula attached.

The title of the poem explicitly invites comparison with "Toads" in "The Less Deceived" (1955). The energy in the earlier poem is in the form of a protest at the time work takes up- six days per week- and how little time it leaves for chasing our dreams ("the fame and the girl and the money"). Its conclusion is that work is a necessary (though overbearing) counterbalance to self-indulgence; delayed gratification is, on the whole, a good thing. In both poems, there is no choice between good or fulfilling work and bad work or drudgery, but both poems articulate our tendency to desire structure, meaning and direction or purpose as an element of our mental well-being, as well as the anarchic, id-like wish to rebel against it.

It may be useful to read "The Whitsun Weddings" as a poetic expression of the battle to contain and suppress the id, the uncontrolled and anti-social instinct to please oneself, without regard to others. It is there in "Self's the Man", and the tension between the drives of the individual and the controlling influence of social norms is a source of dramatic tension in many of the poems; Storyville versus the cathedrals and churches of Chichester and elsewhere.

Water

The first person narrative voice is at its strongest so far, in this short poem, the eleventh in the collection.

The lexis of religious observance (a religion/ church/ liturgy/ devout/ congregate) combines with the lexis of water (water/ fording/ dry/ sousing/ drench/ raise a glass of water).

Line 2 introduces the idea that religions are a "construct"- something built, something artificial, not the expression of an underlying spiritual truth. The fact that construction is usually out of hard materials- concrete, bricks, metal, glass, wood etc- makes the statement that water would be useful seem a surprise, and an unconvincing one.

Stanzas 2 and 3 may allude to the practices of the Baptist Church. They focus on the concept that worshippers would themselves be made soaking wet as a routine part of a church service.

If we have so far become used to Larkin writing poems in "solid" forms, with rhyme and stanzas creating a fixed frame, this poem is more "liquid", with an irregular 4 lines in the final stanza, and lines ranging from 4 to 7 syllables in length.

The apparent half-rhyme in the opening two lines is contradicted subsequently; apart from the repetition of "water" at the end of lines 3 and 11, the only other ghost of a rhyme is church/drench (lines 4, 9).

This odd aversion to the solidity of rhymes matches the poem's title. Oddness extends to some of the word choices in the poem- "images" (line 8), "furious" (9), "different" (6) and "endlessly" (13) all seem arbitrary and lacking in context.

"The east" is the origin of more than one religion- Christianity and Islam, for example- so that the final stanza conflates different types of belief and categorises them as one and the same. What do we expect to "raise in the east"? Ourselves? A Saviour? Some sacred artefact? What Larkin's narrator would raise is a matter-of-fact, down-to-earth glass of water, which is transparent yet contains, to borrow from Keats, "all ye need to know"- beauty and truth (and life itself). While the New Testament may have related Jesus turning water into wine, there is no such transformation here; water remains obstinately water, and Larkin uses other poems to argue that, while some of us attribute mystical value to religious buildings, they are really as anodyne as water is among other drinking materials.

The poem feels like a debunking of the construct of religion, with its rituals, its artefacts and its symbolism; and an accusation that religion has no more substance than a glass of water, because you could construct a religion out of this simple thing and turn it into an object of reverence.

It is almost as if, as we cluster or congregate around the glass of mystical water in the final stanza, the narrator is saying "I caught you at it!"; and as if, having done that, he refuses to exploit our herd mentality further (though he could). We have already seen the hysteria of the herd in "Faith Healing".

If "Faith Healing" analysed the need of women to feel loved, and "Toads Revisited" analysed the need of men to find validation in work, this poem analyses the appeal of the construct of religion. Faith Healers, Work and Religion are, it seems, an unholy trinity, but each has a role to play in meeting the psychological needs of the human being, because there is no deeper spiritual truth to be found in human experience (see the poem "Ignorance" later in the sequence).

A further possibility is that the idea of building a religion out of a glass of water is a sideswipe at T S Eliot's "The Waste Land" (1922), the poster-poem of modernism (Larkin's tastes tended towards the traditional), which uses aridity as a metaphor for the decline of spirituality in the western world after the carnage of the First World War ("rock without water"). Just as Larkin does not accept that a religious belief is necessary, to water the arid soul, he does not believe that modernism is a useful and fruitful construct for literature.

The Whitsun Weddings

The poem draws on the historical fact that for one weekend each year the cost of a marriage license was suspended; this encouraged poor families to choose that weekend for their weddings. It is a particular Saturday in May.

The poem was composed over a long period, so its thesis- that it records a specific, single train journey (from Hull to London) is an imaginative intensifying of a trip Larkin made on three separate occasions, including the Whitsun Saturday of May 28th 1955.

The first stanza describes the slow start to the train journey; there is a sense of a gradual gathering of pace, and a latent intensity in the heat (sunlit/ hot/ tall heat, line 11) and in the repetition of "all" (three times in line 5, then in line 11). The first person singular (I and my, lines 1 and 4) soon alters to the plural "we" (6, 9); this elides the distinction between the narrator as observer and narrator as participant. This poem is perhaps the closest Larkin comes to being involved in an actual, real wedding, but only vicariously.

The start of the journey is related with a precise imprecision (about one-twenty; three-quarters-empty); those repetitions of "all" are a little like the sound you hear as the train you are on passes some series of objects in quick succession. The list of three quick images (a street, windscreens, the fish-dock) yields to the slower, broader sounds of the adjectives attached to the river (Humber) in line 9.

The regularity and predictability of the sound of the train on the track is reflected in the regularity of the rhyme scheme- ABABCDECDC – and the rhythm; apart from line 4 in each stanza, the poem is in iambic pentameters throughout, unhurried, relaxedly purposeful.

Stanza 2 serves to heighten the reader's senses. There is a list of six images (farms, cattle, canals, a hothouse, hedges, dismantled cars) and an emphasis both on the feeling of heat- "the tall heat", "hothouse"- and the scents and smells of the hot, heavy upholstery on the train seats, and the smell of grass. This is an imaginative leap; the fields are far enough away from train tracks for it to be difficult for us to inhale grass aromas, or so you would think.

Much of the furniture of the poem is common to "Here" also- industrial shadows/industrial froth; fishy-smelling/ smell of grass; silence like heat/ the tall heat; high as hedges/hedges dipped; fast-shadowed/ short-shadowed; fishy-smelling/smelt the fish dock/ river's low presence/ river's level drifting; skies/ sky; waters quicken/ water meet.

The tone in "The Whitsun Weddings" is less lyrical, less detached, because of the use of the pronouns "I" and "we" which alternate; "Here" was narrated in the third person. Now, after the end-stopped first two stanzas, we have to wait till the end of the poem for a full stop and a stanza end to coincide. The description of the wedding-parties on the station platforms runs from line 27 to line 55.

That description moves, like a camera, from one group to another- girls, fathers, mothers, an uncle, girls, fresh couples, children, father, the women, girls. There is an odd effect here; the narrator identifies himself more as a participant, using "we" or "us" in lines 27, 28, 30, 48 and 57, yet much of the choice of detail and the language of the description is sarcastic and even demeaning- the "parody of fashion" and "jewellery-substitutes" are not the real thing, but a pretence, a pale imitation. We discover the reasons for this attitude in lines 55 and 67. The act of getting married is not a religious celebration or a religious ritual but a "wounding", because it cuts you off from "the others" you can now "never meet"; the irrevocability of marriage, its randomness and the way it narrows down the remainder of your life, makes the institution, for the narrator, oxymoronic, "A happy funeral".

In fact, this part of the poem is full of the lexis of death (destroys/ the shade/ the end/ waving goodbye/ survived/ an end/ all down the line (like a battlefield trench)/ the last/ departing/ funeral/ gouts (of blood)/ long shadows/ died/ done/ out of sight). While the poem deals with the time-limited opportunity for a cheap wedding, it also implies that the future life of the newly-weds is equally circumscribed; there is no joy here. These couples can anticipate the awkward silences of "Talking in Bed".

Larkin himself may not have seen this; in an interview in 1980, he challenged the assertion that unhappiness beckoned these fresh couples, but the poem is infused with his own circumspection (bordering on paranoia) about the impossibility/ difficulty of choosing the right marriage partner.

You can find this in the poem "Places, Loved Ones" in "The Less Deceived"; and in "Maiden Name", where the narrator defines adopting your spouse's name as "losing shape and meaning less", and as becoming weighed down by the baggage of someone else, which drags you down and erodes your individuality over time.

The final two and a half stanzas gather speed (We hurried/ we raced) but the end of the poem is an anti-climax; perhaps the honeymoons of these young couples will be, too. The narrator frames the shared experience of the journey as a "frail…coincidence", and he contrasts his own thoughts with the thoughtlessness of the couples.

Remaining unmarried, London is, for him, "spread out in the sun"- an opportunity to "meet others". He is relieved that he can keep open the sense, at least, that he has access to a world of different potential intimacies, instead of tying himself to just one.

As the train slows to a halt, the atmosphere becomes darker and even claustrophobic, as though we watch "an arrow-shower"- the aiming and the paths of a large number of arrows, "loosed with….power" but falling to earth because of the power of gravity.

We are all going to the terminus of death, the poem seems to say; the unknowable puzzle is whether it is better to do this in the company of another person, or as an individual.

The same speculation informs "Dockery & Son" and "Self's the Man", and the recurring reluctance of Larkin, and his narrators, to commit- or perhaps the active, though sometimes reluctant, decision to remain single- has a certain modernity to it, as the institution of marriage has gone on to have a less powerful hold over succeeding generations.

Self's the Man

The opening line refers to the popular rhyme "For he's a jolly good fellow", a wedding, birthday or drinking song, where the sentiment goes unthought about, unchallenged, and a group of men show solidity with each other.

This poem reaches the same conclusion, eventually, in its thesis that men behave towards women in a generally similar way (and they don't criticise themselves for it)- out of self-interest, whether or not this leads them, individually, into marriage. It begins by extolling the apparent selflessness of the married man (Arnold is based on Arthur Wood, a library colleague whom Larkin was fond of ridiculing in his letters).

However, line 3 undermines the integrity of the married man, with its contention that the protagonist here married an unnamed "woman to stop her getting away".

This has echoes of Larkin's pursuit, as a young man, of Ruth Bowman, and it suggests that a fear of being lonely drives men towards commitments they may regret later.

Arnold, the protagonist of the poem, is presented with comic bathos but without much sympathy. He has made his bed and he must lie in it; his commitments, as a married man, are to give up- or devote- all his spare time, and all he can earn, to the needs of his growing family, and the demands of his wife (for DIY around the house) and his mother in law.

Larkin himself seems to have recoiled from the faint scent of any domestic or economic responsibility towards anyone (at least until he came to look after Monica Jones in the last years of his life).

The narrator here is like the narrator in "Mr Bleaney"; both voices recognise that what separates them from an emasculated failure- a life as Bleaney or Arnold- is paper-thin. Bleaney's human connections were minimal and he leaves no legacy; Arnold's existence, devoid of any time to himself, will be marked by little more than a screw in the wall.

The irony is that, in "Mr Bleaney", the narrator is aware of the fact that he is, in a sense, becoming Bleaney; in "Self's the Man", the narrator is confident he won't make Arnold's mistake, but he acknowledges, in the final line of the poem, that his own self-centredness and the loneliness it leads to may drive him mad.

Perhaps Arnold underestimated what he could stand- his fear of a lonely irrelevance misled him into jumping out of the frying pan into the fire, and an equally unsatisfactory loneliness, surrounded by relatives by marriage. His wife's family are very present, but his own is completely absent from the poem, implying that the decisive act of marrying may be a substitute for having a social structure of your own parents and siblings.

Like so many of Larkin's poems, this one uses the persona of a detached narrator who is on the outside, looking in, to offer a sceptical, knowing and even cynical view of marriage.

His argument is that the companionship marriage seems to offer involves giving up your access to your real self.

In his 1961 poem, "Love", Larkin asserts that putting someone else first all the time is like defying gravity- it breaks a natural law, and therefore can't be done. The poem "Wants" in "The Less Deceived" observes the strength of "the wish to be alone", and in the earlier poem "Best Society" he had spoken of solitude as a natural and innate aspect of being alive. His consistent view is that to be alone is not the same as being anti-social; in fact, having time to ourselves is necessary if we are to be ourselves, however unsatisfactory isolation from others may seem.

Arnold, according to the narrator, married for his own (selfish) ends, and pleased himself as well as his friends in doing so. As in "The Whitsun Weddings", there is an implied concession here that marriage does no particular harm as a social construct; but implicit in it is a "falling", a diminishing of the energy and powers of the individual.

In terms of its structure, the poem is in two halves. The first deals with the drudgery of Arnold's domestic routine, and specifically his poverty in having no time for himself. We might expect the second half of the poem to dramatise the narrator's life in the equivalent terms- perhaps drinking a serene coffee- but it denies us this, perhaps because that would reveal a Bleaney-like emptiness and isolation. Instead, it turns to musing on the flaw in Arnold's motivation, implying that Arnold has brought his plight on himself by behaving dishonourably, and- according to the final stanza- without real self-knowledge. The narrative voice becomes the most interesting element of the poem, poised awkwardly between smugness and a sort of guiltiness. The subject matter of the poem- the motivation for marriage- will be explored further in "Dockery & Son".

Take One Home for the Kiddies

Framed like a poem by Blake, in its childlike simplicity of form (ABBA), this poem uses Blake-like symbolism, to make the life and death of rabbits/ hamsters/ guinea-pigs (the species is not specified) a symbol for human life and death.

Again like Blake, the poem presents a tension between its apparently innocuous surface and the darkness just beneath it. The pets (seen in a pet shop, perhaps) are "living toys", but in no time- in the space of three lines- they are dead. Meanwhile, the conditions of their lives, as they are related in the first stanza, all convey a sense of discomfort, while the four hammer blows of "no" in line 3 emphasise the absence of anything comforting.

The animals have no family ties ("no dam") and no control over their own lives; they are merely the playthings of children, who do have mothers of their own. If the newly- acquired pet commands any interest because it is "novel", that illusion of care or being cared for "soon wears off".

Translated into human terms, the view of the poem is that we go from being in the shop window to being adopted, but any warmth we feel when someone picks us out and takes us home is just an interlude before we die (which may happen sooner than we think). The shoebox as a metaphor for a coffin, together with the metaphor of toys and play, is grim, wry, and devoid of either pity or self-pity.

The poem is therefore a short philosophical reflection on the emptiness and essential loneliness (not to say misery) of life. By using the analogy of a rabbit, and without anthropomorphising it, the poem avoids mawkishness. By dressing it up as a nursery rhyme, and then giving it the Roald Dahl treatment, Larkin alerts us to the grit in the oyster; the existential problem of the nagging question, why are we here?

In his previous collection, "The Less Deceived", Larkin uses cattle and horses as the protagonists in poems which make observations about human life (a technique used also by Ted Hughes); he will do this with animals again, later in this collection, in "First Sight".

Days

It is very unusual to find an asymmetrical poem in this collection. "Water" concluded with an extra line (three tercets and a quatrain). Now, we have a poem in two stanzas, of six lines, then four. These two poems lack a formal rhyme scheme; this, too, makes them stand apart from the other thirteen poems we have examined so far. Of the remaining poems, only "Reference Back" has stanzas of varying lengths, and it is regulated by rhyme; only "Afternoons" is unconcerned with rhyme, and it is in a rigid stanza structure.

The poem hinges on a "conceit", or supposition, that days are not only made up of time, and therefore non-physical, but that they have a physical location- they are places, "where we live"; like our domestic surroundings, they are "to be happy in".

Days are personified, too; they wake us, as though they are the early riser in our household.

The poem poses two questions, in lines 1 and 6. It answers neither of them explicitly, but in the very failure to answer, it still provides some answers. Days are the cells or molecules of our lives, and they are units of time. To ask what they are for is to ask what we are for, or what purpose our lives serve.

The priest and the doctor are brought into the scenery of the poem only when we raise this question of the purpose or meaning of our existence; they come "running" because the very asking of those questions generates distress or some kind of spiritual or health crisis. There is no third stanza in which a prescription or cure is administered. Neither can the faith healer or the paramedics in ambulances address the underlying (terminal) illness which afflicts those they minister to.

The "long coats" in line 9 may be an invitation to relate this poem to the long coats in line 15 of "Toads Revisited", where the people who wear them are rummaging in rubbish; in the stuff others have discarded as rubbish.

The tramps in "Toads Revisited" are doing nothing useful; by extension, neither are these priests and doctors.

The noun "fields" has a broader significance when it (rarely) appears in this set of poems with their largely urban settings. In "Here", the fields are dry and rough; in "MCMXIV", they foreshadow death, and they are part of an uncaring, indifferent landscape. In these poems overall, fields are an unchanging, permanent feature of the landscape and they are indifferent to the plight of the human being, let alone the span of an individual life.

In "The Less Deceived", Larkin's philosophical observations included the theory that, beneath our psychological need to be alone, we have a death wish, a "desire of oblivion" (in "Wants"). In "Next, Please", he had remarked that we have a tendency to think that our desires will be fulfilled in the future, but we are continually disappointed, and never gratified; the ship which we think is approaching the harbour for us does not come "to unload/ All good into our lives", but to summon us to die. In this context, being woken up daily by time, to ponder the same unanswerable questions, is uncomfortable and unwelcome- though less unwelcome than not being alive at all.

Like so many of the poems, "Days" accepts, without bitterness, fear or joy, the condition of being alive- the helplessness, the dissatisfaction, and the difficulty of trying to assert control over our own lives when nothing really works- faith healing, work, marriage, intimacy.

Days are the ingredients of life and "life is slow dying" ("Nothing To Be Said"); so, when we reach the end of the poem, or the end of our days, the priest may come to administer the last rites, and the doctor may come to write the death certificate, but neither they nor anyone else can tell us what our days, or our lives, are really "for".

We will still be trying to find the answers when our time is over (line 4). Or, rather, we will want to find a way of "solving" it- as if it were a particularly difficult and frustrating clue in a cryptic crossword.

MCMXIV

In a stylistic echo of "Here", with its deployment of the key word "here" three times in the final (fourth) stanza, this poem stresses, through repetition, the key words "never" and "innocence" in the same way, in the final stanza.

The poem therefore contemplates the irreversible change the First World War wrought. In literary terms, it provoked the genesis of Modernism, in a world in which religious belief now seemed far less sustainable or credible. In social terms, it destroyed families, because, out of a total UK population of 46 million in 1914, 886000 British combatants would be killed. The August Bank Holiday in line 8 was 3rd; Britain declared war on Germany on 4th, and, from 7th, in response to Lord Kitchener's recruitment drive, 33,000 men aged between 19 and 30 volunteered for active service, thinking that the War would be over by Christmas.

The poem is in a single, panoramic sentence; an extension of the long opening three stanza sentence in "Here". The semi-colons at the end of each of the first three stanzas help to make this visual journey a little like the train journey in "Here", with its sequence of urban, suburban and rural scenes. But where "Here" sets its closing seascape apart, as a safe haven of solitude, away from the collective or general experience, through the full stops and new sentences in its final stanza, "MCMXIV" makes no exceptions; there is no-one alive in 1914 whose innocence is intact after this day. The word "all" infects each of the first three stanzas (lines 7, 16, 18).

The language of the poem serves the aim of drawing a line under the "past" (line 33). We have dynamic verbs in the present tense (standing/ grinning/ not caring/ flowering/shadowing/ leaving/ lasting) and verbs in the past tense (stretched/called/hazed/ changed), and markers of time and space- archaic/ after/behind/ before/ since/ never---again.

The similes in stanza 1 are not descriptive; they highlight the dramatic irony that the bank holiday mood of play and larks, and the innocent pleasure of watching cricket or football, is about to come to an abrupt end.

The third stanza has an ominous quality, because of the personification of the fields (not caring) and the wheat (restless silence), and the link with Domesday- the violent resistance against the French in 1066, or the day we meet our fate.

The ambiguity half-conceals a dramatic irony, and so does the phrase "tin advertisement"- an advertisement on a tin, and Kitchener's fateful appeal for men to volunteer to join the army and be issued with tin helmets. The fields of France will be the fields of doom; the silence of the wheat here is restless, like the men themselves, who are cheerfully excited.

Nowhere else in this collection does Larkin fix on a historical event, except where it is incidental to his personal life. That is not the case here- he had not been born in 1914. So it is superficially odd that we find such an atypical poem right at the heart of the series (sixteenth out of the thirty-two poems).

The explanation must be that he traces the fraying of the fabric of English society to the First World War- the imminent threat of the ending of "thousands of marriages" (through widowhood) and the loss of innocence, which has engendered in his narrative voices and personae this disengagement with the religious, the spiritual, and the need to conform to the institutions and values of the past.

The world he has grown up in is by nature individualistic and defensive. With innocence goes optimism and naivete; so that if there is a mildly nihilistic tone to his characters and their experience, it is attributable to that one disastrous event. The poem is, in a way, an explanation of how we come to be "Here", at the start of the collection.

There will have been Whitsun weddings before 1914, too, but the First World War would impress on the generations who grew up after it the sense that life can be brutal and short.

Knowing that life promises dissatisfaction is like living after the Fall of Man (Adam and Eve expelled from the Garden of Eden). Larkin uses the idea of falling to convey this lowering of our horizons, and our inability to reach any higher form of truth or certainty in the post-1914 world.

Talking in Bed

This poem originates in Larkin's relationship with Monica Jones, with whom he was not always honest or candid, particularly about his feelings for Maeve Brennan.

In that sense, the phrase "lying together" may contain an unconscious truth!

For most of us, being "true and kind" is fairly straightforward. For this narrator, it is not.

The legalistic distinction in the final couplet- using a positive form of phraseology or a more opaque, less positive one- conveys a lack of candour which the narrator presents as a lack of clarity in his thinking. The desire not to lie outright, while avoiding telling the whole truth, is known as equivocation; and an equivocal, ineffectual or non-committal attitude is often typical of Larkin (in "Self's the Man", or in the closing "I don't know" of "Mr Bleaney").

The final stanza sets out the great difficulty of being as emotionally close as you are physically close to someone with whom you have a history of intimacy (line 2). The narrator observes that if you are physically distant or isolated it is easier to speak kindly and to disclose your "true" feelings, but when you are physically present (line 9) it is much harder to be honest (we may feel that this is only really difficult if you have something to hide).

The second and third stanzas invite comparison of the content of this poem with "An Arundel Tomb", where the stone memorial is an emblem of intimacy, and where "time passes silently". There, too, a couple lie "supine stationary", but they are observed, memorialised, and they cannot converse.

In "Talking in Bed", the difficulty in finding words which will not make things worse leads the narrator to try to escape, in lines 5-8; the wind shares his lack of ease, his uncomfortable sense of tension building and diffusing; the "dark towns......on the horizon" suggest that the prospect of occupying the same physical space as the person you are intimate with, in a civilised way, is uncomfortable. If being physically close to someone else is being at a "distance from isolation", then isolation seems to become more desirable. The wind could be interpreted as empty talk, too. Its incomplete rest is really the unrest of the narrator- his uneasiness about disclosing himself fully.

In Larkin's poems there is a distinction between loneliness, silence, solitude and isolation. Solitude seems to be a necessary condition for creativity; it is only by standing apart or outside that the poet can make sense of the world around him, and pick the bones out of existence or mortality. Isolation is a condition of being disconnected from other people- Arnold and Mr Bleaney are like this- and it is a psychological, not a physical thing; because you cannot measure the distance to isolation, as it is not a physical place, you cannot measure your distance from it either. Silence and solitude are desirable for

Larkin, and we should see them as a natural part of life; his poems often object to other people's noise. He does not see solitude- the need to be alone- as anti-social, because he tends to see the drive to be sociable as an evasion, a way of hiding from our essential condition of solitude. The company of others is a temporary analgesia for loneliness, but Larkin feels acute anxiety over the question of whether any relationship- and particularly an exclusive one, of marriage- can cure it, or should be thought capable of solving it.

"Talking in Bed" is therefore the most frank and candid of a large group of poems, which all originate in the difficulty (and the ultimate irrelevance) of social constructs, discourse and behaviour. The poignant thing is that what the poem reveals or confesses is divulged to us, the reader, and not to the unspecified bed-companion.

The Large Cool Store

The theme of intimacy extends into this poem, which was prompted by Larkin's visit to a newly opened Marks and Spencer in Hull.

The ABABA rhyme scheme creates a jaunty tone.

The even lines (2, 4, etc) all have nine syllables, except for the shorter final line of the poem, which has eight. The odd-numbered lines have seven or eight. The two lists of colours – the dull colours of day wear and the softer ones of nightwear- each have four constituents (lines 4 and 11). There are two lists of the categories of clothes, in lines 3 and 12. The rhyme of site/night establishes the continuity between daytime occupations and people's nocturnal lives. The workplaces here are unintellectual (no libraries!) and the work is likely to be hard and repetitive.

These blue-collar workers seek out "cheap clothes", for which there is a mass market (line 8). The narrator finds this matter-of-fact and uninteresting, but his interest is captured by the nightwear "past" or beyond the dull, solid, routine garments.

The items which "flounce" in the third stanza are all female garments and they are made of synthetic materials, delicate and opaque.

The first sentence of the poem (lines 1-7) defines the work clothes; the second (lines 8-13) the play clothes. Then we have the longest, final sentence of seven and a half lines, which is much more complex, as the narrator tries to articulate the truth or principle he detects behind the different characters of the different personae the clothes will orchestrate.

The use of the pronouns "they….their…they…..our" is quite obscure; as in "The Whitsun Weddings", pronouns can obscure the difference between the observer and the observed- as well as introducing a mildly voyeuristic tone. Separate/ sort/ synthetic/ new is the lexis of the clothing; "separate" and "share" help to create a sense of clarity and precision in stanza three, but the final stanza is less confident in its analysis, with three "or"s and a distinction between what is real and what seems to be.

This closing sentence is neither an exclamation nor a rhetorical question; even its syntax is preoccupied, exploratory, rather like the process of clothes-shopping.

The narrator expresses his puzzlement that people who work in the "factory, yard and site" should have the imaginative or romantic power to make the erotic clothing feel appropriate to them; they should not be in that market. The narrator explains this surprising conclusion- that the clothes are for these people too- by attributing the demand for them to women, or to the allure of women. It is mainly the men who go out to work in manual jobs; women (or "love") are "unearthly", mistresses of illusion, the objects of male fantasy.

This narrator wonders at the idea that the women who inhabit the "low terraced houses" have the capacity to engage with and encourage the "unreal" male appetite for fantasy, new materials and soft pastel colours in the bedroom. The final word of the poem- "ecstasies"- contrasts with the plain, grey workaday routine in the opening lines of the poem.

It may also be an oblique reference to John Donne's poem "The Extasie", which explores the power and intensity of sex in an established relationship. Donne dramatizes ecstasy as a spiritual state, a connection between people, in which the "abler soul....defects of lonelinesse controules". If we apply this to Larkin's poem, which is a legitimate approach because he, like Donne, is interested in the "unearthly" or transformational quality of sexual love (though without Donne's frankness), Larkin's narrator is not thinking of women as sex objects (the characterisation of "women" as a group is too vague for that anyway) but reflecting on their emotional hold over the men they live with.

We know that Larkin's principal love interest, Monica Jones, sent him photos of herself dressed in ways which he found erotically stimulating; this poem may originate in a recurrent attempt on his part to explain or understand the nature of that stimulus, which is not merely visual but also emotional.

He may have found it reassuring to discover that department stores are catering for a mass market in lingerie and nightwear which suggests that he is surrounded by people who share his psychology- even if, to judge by their jobs and their homes, he is surprised to make the connection between himself and them.

A Study of Reading Habits

Here, we find yet another distinctive narrative voice. This one is volatile- there is a sharp difference between the start and the end of the poem- and violent, or at least aggressive, in the middle stanza, although the grimly comical tone takes the edge off this.

The ABCBAC rhyme scheme implies that the narrator has a tight grip on his world, but the balance in the form of the poem, and its cheerful metre, only serves to exaggerate the many ways in which this narrator is out of control.

His persona is that of a cartoon character, a hero quick with his fists- like Batman- (stanza 1); a demonic antihero or vampire/ sexual predator- a cartoon villain (stanza 2); and, in stanza three, a minor character, who has been pushed to the side of the story, because his lack of true heroism has revealed itself (like the young mothers, pushed to the side of their own lives, in "Afternoons", he is merely a spectator).

When we reach the end of the poem, and the disclosure that the imaginative world in which this narrator has constructed for himself the identity he wanted, only to find it a failure, we feel slightly sorry for him; his frustration leads to an extreme disillusionment with a life in which he seems incapable of effective social interaction. He rejects literature as reflective of life, in favour of the injunction to "get stewed" (turn to drink). This implies that life needs pain relief, and that literature cannot provide it, in middle age.

The second stanza is perhaps confessional (the pun of lark/Larkin and the "inch-thick specs" may be a kind of autograph); it concedes an excitable interest in the dark/sex/evil, while trying to disguise or trivialise it in the fancy dress of a vampire. The narrator seems to want to be a vampire, or thinks he is one, or pretends to be one. In all three stanzas he fails- spectacularly- to behave in an appropriate or effective way, and he seems to have a predilection for violence (right hook/ clubbed/ ripping). It is as if, while presenting himself in an unflattering light, he challenges us to condemn him, knowing that we will not, because we can see, through the pattern of the narrative, that his emotional impairments have always been part of his personality, from childhood onwards.

While the pronouns in the first two stanzas indicate a strong egomania (my/my/I/my/my/me and my/ I/I), the "I" is omitted in stanza three (I don't read much…… get stewed) in favour of "the" (the dude/ the girl/ the hero/ the chap/ the store). The reading matter here is the Western, or American pulp fiction.

It is not reading which has ruined the narrator's eyes- rather, it is an unrealistic outlook on life, and social maladjustment, which has ruined his optimism as well as his clarity of vision. That unhelpful perspective has not come from the influence of the (non-realistic) fiction he has chosen to read- it is more a case of choosing material to read which has always helped him to avoid dealing with the real world.

It is grimly ironic that a librarian and poet should be so dismissive of the written word, but Larkin goes on to express his frustration about the lack of revelation in literature in "Ignorance", and the obscurity of "truth" in "Send No Money", while the word "unsatisfactory" dominates "Reference Back". As we work through the collection, we can detect a growing sense of frustration; is the artist's solitude really worth it? Is the gnomic persona of the poet just another fancy dress, an attempt at becoming the hero, when in fact you are too cowardly or too ineffectual to make a dynamic contribution to your readers' lives?

The poems, as a set, present many variations on the persona of the narrator; all of them are discontented, detached, and more or less unsuccessful or unhappy. The single poem which experiences any joy is "For Sidney Bechet". The poems turn, increasingly, to their narrators' past, to the idealised pre-1914 or childhood world, and finally to the Arundel tomb, for answers, but there are no conclusive or reassuring answers to be found.

As Bad as a Mile

The title of this poem is a piece of ellipsis- it refers to the proverb "A miss is as good as a mile", and then replaces "good" with its opposite, "bad", because it is about "failure", not success. The meaning of the proverb is that if you miss what you aim to achieve or hit, the margin by which you fail is irrelevant.

The poem comprises two triplets (AAA/ BBB) which trace back the failure to get the apple core into the waste paper basket to the point before the apple first started to be eaten.

The uneaten apple is on some level a symbol of the human condition before the concept of original sin had originated (Adam and Eve in the Garden of Eden). The poem makes the point that the discarded core- all that is left of the apple- does not miss the waste paper bin randomly, because it goes astray out of the thrower's hand; the missing is implicit in even taking the apple to your desk in the first place.

This doctrine of deterioration- everything is rotten to the core, and things tend to get worse and worse- is presented here in a "calm" way; it is accepted without a hint of protest, or resistance, because you can't resist the irresistible.

In isolation, this short poem may seem irrelevant, but we need to be conscious that we are reading a collection of poems, where each one helps to inform the meanings of the rest. Home becomes sadder; pets die; once "life is half over", we become conscious of our own mortality; and, in the (Arundel) tomb, "time" transfigures us into "untruth" and oblivion. Life is a process of slow dying, of turning away from music and books; as we see before us the "bestial visor"- the impossibility of living graciously and aesthetically- there is "nothing to be said".

Such a pessimistic outlook is explicable if the whole world is going to hell in a handcart- if life is just a process of loosening our grip and waiting for "what is left to come" ("Ambulances"). This poem gives us a clue about the philosophy behind the tone of resignation, the apparent equanimity, with which Larkin's late- 1950s characters accept their collective fate.

Ambulances

Enclosed spaces of various kinds appear throughout this collection; Mr Bleaney's one hired box, the Arundel tomb, the low terraced houses, bed, the shoe-box, litter-baskets, a stable, a locked room, an unsatisfactory room, frames, that small cube. But they are at their most concentrated and claustrophobic in the ambulances here- closed like confessionals/ fastened doors/ inside a room. It is worse to be locked inside an ambulance than to be outside the locked door of your student rooms- because you are no longer free to go elsewhere.

Unsurprisingly, the lexical field of death is woven into the structure- glossy grey (like a gravestone)/ a plaque/ come to rest/ stowed/ lies just under/ permanent/ soul/ distress/ borne away/ deadened/ sudden shut/ loss/ at an end/ at last/ lie unreachable. These ambulances never bring back anyone who has been discharged from hospital; they only carry away and stow or store those who will never return. The sight of an ambulance does not reassure onlookers- it simply reminds them that nothing can be done for the patient, and that they too face the same fate, because "all streets in time are visited" for this harvesting of the almost dead.

The idea that "emptiness" can be "solving" (line 13) is a striking one. In "Days", "solving that question" brought the priest and the doctor; the question was the meaning of life, or its lack of meaning- its emptiness, which we choose to disregard, as far as we can, because to reflect on it would make us ill or drive us mad. Seeing an ambulance, and in particular seeing the stricken patient put inside, with the stark contrast of red blankets (blood, which keeps us alive) and "a wild white face" (death), makes it impossible to ignore the uncomfortable truth "Days" confronted us with.

The patient is immobile and helpless, and the ambulance doors are fastened, so that he/she becomes dulled to distance (in space, and then in time)- this foreshadows the transfiguration in "An Arundel Tomb".

There may be other cross-references within the collection too. Lying, exchanging love, but unreachable, reminds us of "Talking in Bed". "Families" connote with the named characters Dockery, Arnold, Bleaney, and their meaningless lives. "Fashions"- meaning habits first, and clothes second- relates to the maladjustment and dysfunction of "A Study of Reading Habits" and to "The Large Cool Store" (aka the morgue).

The undifferentiated women and children in lines 7-8 are the same as those in "Afternoons"- spectators, not participants- and in "Take One Home for the Kiddies"- those about to bury a dead pet.

The language constructs a sense of closure or finality- closed/ permanent/ fastened/ away/ shut/ at an end/ last/ let go. In "MCMXIV", the shops were shut, symbolising the fact that we cannot preserve the past, and that some things or relationships suddenly become closed to us (by death). There is no repetition in "Ambulances". It involves a single journey from which there is no coming back.

Larkin deploys a large battery of (twenty) adjectives and alliteration (thirteen instances). The final use of alliteration- "dulls to distance"- creates a sense of poignancy because, as the ambulance recedes, out of sight, so do the loosened family ties, and so too does the momentary awareness of our own mortality. The onlookers pity, not the dying patient, but "their own distress".

The ambulance's visit, too, is only of momentary interest- the cooking smells, the shopping, and the traffic continue to function (Carol Ann Duffy makes the same point about our careless attachment to our domestic routines, in he midst of other people's deaths, in "War Photographer").

The verse is in iambic tetrameters throughout, with a rhyme scheme ABCBCA. The effect is that all human experience will enact this scene, in its own way; no one, in any street, is exempt from the visitation of a final illness. The poem is a painting of the observation in "Nothing To Be Said"- life is slow dying, for these children and women too (though it is closer to hand for those stowed in the ambulance).

The Importance of Elsewhere

This poem has an ABAB rhyme scheme and is in iambic pentameters. It is autobiographical, in that Larkin refers to his time in Northern Ireland, and specifically in Belfast. He lists some of the differences which gave Belfast its distinctive character- differences which meant that he was recognised (partly via his accent) as a stranger. Now that he is in Hull, he cannot see himself as so different; the social norms are his own, because Hull is in England, so he cannot opt out of them in the same way.

The last line of the poem sums up its thesis. Underwriting is a technical term from the world of insurance- risk is underwritten, so that the individual who is insured does not have to worry if something goes wrong. Without underwriting, risk may be assessed incorrectly, or, possibly, not at all; so the narrator is saying that if he wants to be critical of his fellow- English, he will implicate himself.

For a poet, this is an important point. Larkin's position and voice is largely that of the outsider; he needs a degree of detachment, and a certain license to criticise attitudes he observes in the culture or society he operates within. His previous collection of poems, "The Less Deceived", originated in his time in Belfast. Although he was not lonely in his personal life at this stage, Larkin presents a narrator who is- an alter ego who is anxious about whether the isolation of the observer, the deliberate refusal to engage as other people do, is worth it. If the poetry he wishes to write depends on detachment or "strangeness", will he be able to maintain that perspective of separation now that he is living again in England?

"Elsewhere" has indeed now been abbreviated to just its last four letters- "here"- in the opening poem of this collection.

Sunny Prestatyn

Thirteen of the thirty-two poems in "The Whitsun Weddings" are in three stanzas; this is one. Its rhyme scheme is ABCABDCD. Some of the rhymes are either surprising (Prestatyn/satin, scrawls/balls) or banal (poster/a, March/crotch).

The poem brings together two of Larkin's particular interests- advertising posters (which he develops in "Essential Beauty"), and the sexualised visual stimulus he finds emanating from women (which he develops in "Wild Oats").

The narrative in the poem is the progressive defacing of the poster-girl- first, the poster is made sexually obscene, in stanza 2, and then it is vandalised, violently. The narrator does not make a judgment or pass comment on this; he merely records it, in a detached manner, which implies that he condones it, or is at least fascinated by it, without feeling that such behaviour should be disapproved of.

The girl on the poster is personified, from the start, where she laughs. "Slapped up" in line 9 is literally true- glue and brushes would fix the poster in place on its hoarding- but it also connotes (sexual) violence, only four poems on from the second stanza of "A Study of Reading Habits". Line 21 is the sort of comment a priest might make in a funeral eulogy- as if she was a real person.

To the narrator, the girl is very real- his gaze lingers on her erogenous body parts and "tautened", body-hugging clothes. The description is generalised- she has no distinguishing features, only the female form.

The language of the description is male, blunt, lacking in anything other than a vaguely pornographic satisfaction. The single sentence which occupies lines 10-20 is almost breathless in its enthusiasm or admiration for what it describes.

Some of the details in the final stanza are notable. The final line announces that the next poster on the board is an injunction to "Fight Cancer"- not, presumably, the so-called cancer of depersonalising women, or the insidious "spread" of pornography, but the deadly illnesses we are familiar with!

The 1964 publication date coincides with the patriarchal male attitudes towards women prior to the "swinging 60s". A backlash against this came with the sexual revolution prompted by the contraceptive pill (available to British women from late 1961) which led to the genesis of feminism because it empowered women to have more and safer sex if they wished to do so. The historical context needs to be applied, when we consider whether the poem ends with a critique of male attitudes in which the sexual exploitation of women is taken as a law of nature.

"Titch Thomas" is a colloquial or slang term for "small penis". The implication of this (non-essential) detail is that the crude graffiti artist who defaces the poster has an inferiority complex and is intimidated by female sexuality.

There is, however, a caesura at the end of the second stanza- a voyeuristic lingering on the image of the girl "astride". The defacing of the girl's face (line 11) and the artistic flourishes which exaggerate her sexual objectification intensify the sense of the narrator's erotic gratification in observing and then recording it.

The word "hunk" in line 5 evokes a hunk of bread, something that can be torn and devoured, to satisfy the most basic appetite. The "palms" in line 6 have no place in Prestatyn (they belong in Hawaii or the Mediterranean if they are trees). Kneeling and palms also suggest an attitude of prayer; the subliminal advertising message is that Prestatyn will be sexy and sunny, with its welcoming girls.

In Larkin's previous collection of poems, "The Less Deceived" (1955), perhaps the most powerful poem is "Next, Please"- a devastating poem about "disappointment", which argues that we continually dream that our boat is coming in/ our dreams are about to be realised; but that the ship which symbolises the satisfaction of all our deepest desires never anchors- it just sails past. That ship is characterised as having a "figurehead with golden tits". Female breasts are thus a motif for emotional as well as sexual pleasure and satisfaction in Larkin's poetry.

"Sunny Prestatyn" leaves us with the sense that, just as the claims for the Welsh holiday resort are exaggerated- in fact, a lie- the so-called dream of sex without the complications of responsibility is an uncomfortable one.

The poem follows Larkin's poem about Belfast, where he had enjoyed a no strings attached relationship with Patsy Strang, while extricating himself from Ruth Bowman; it also owes something to the character of his long-distance relationship with Monica Jones. Larkin may have felt that sex made relationships which would otherwise be pure and alluring into something more manipulative and exploitative.

Like "A Study of Reading Habits", "Sunny Prestatyn" explores the thin line between fantasy and reality; between idealising and defacing your idols; between the ego and the id. Larkin finds it difficult to imagine that the people of Hull have much use for Marks and Spencers' risqué lingerie. His male narrators are typical of the late 1950s, in their lack of understanding or recognition of the emotional value of sex; they are less interested in what it does to you than in how it can occupy your imagination, as a diversion.

First Sight

Because this poem focuses on animals, it is reminiscent of "Take One Home for the Kiddies". Its rhyme scheme is deceptively simple- ABABACC. Lambs normally connote springtime gambols; however, the conventional form of this poem belies its harsh content.

These lambs are born in winter, into an actively hostile world (vast unwelcome/ sunless glare/ cold) which leaves them "bleating/ stumbling/wretched".

The second stanza contrasts with the first. Under the snow, it tells us, there is, albeit hidden from view, "Earth's immeasurable surprise"- something the opposite of snow, which will "wake and grow", and which is impossible for them to "grasp".

Because what "it" is is not specified, the poem is highly ambiguous. If we read it as a conventional pastoral poem, which celebrates the peace and safety of the countryside, "it" will be a warm, dry Spring, much more hospitable than the unwelcoming winter.

The alternative, less obvious- and therefore more interesting- interpretation is that, as in the poem about rabbits, what awaits the lambs is a cruel death in the Spring. The orthodox mutation from winter to spring is hardly an "immeasurable surprise"- it happens every year, without fail. The idea that you will survive a cold snowy winter, only to be slaughtered in the Spring, is. The snow has no deliberate intention to kill them; the taste and demand for meat (lamb) does.

Is it a coincidence that this poem is placed immediately after "Sunny Prestatyn", a poem in which girls were represented as bread, fodder for slaughter, an object of appetite, treated as a commodity, depersonalised, and subjected (as a species) to unprovoked violence, "a knife/ Or something to stab right through"?

The unpleasant and unexpected surprise is therefore that, as a lamb, you will be separated from your mother, and that, if you negotiate your initial wretchedness, you will bleat and stumble through your life before being taken away to die. We could say that this short poem is a restatement and a distillation of "Mr Bleaney" plus "Ambulances"- or, perhaps, a number of other combinations which you can divine for yourself.

Both this poem, "Take One Home for the Kiddies", and "At Grass" (in "The Less Deceived") use animals and their lives, not for their own sake, but to comment on aspects of our human lives, and to imbue the process of ageing and moving towards death (slow dying) as something inevitable, harsh and pitiable, but- because it is absolutely universal- not to be grieved over, in advance.

Dockery and Son

This narrator is in some senses Larkin himself; born in 1922, a graduate of Oxford University, unmarried, not a house owner, a traveller by train (not by car).

The title of the poem "Dockery and Son" suggests a commercial partnership- you will see such names on the side of removals lorries, plumbers, butchers, painters etc.

The setting for the poem is a college memorial service for Dockery, but that event occupies only the first ten lines of this 48-line poem. In the third stanza, the narrator's self-obsession and self-interest begins to assert itself- in philosophical terms this is an expression of existential angst. The narrator will consider whether the conventional aspects of a life- family, children, permanent relationships- are desirable; is the path of our own life simply a random one?

Our motivations, as individual human beings, are distinctive, and they must have come from our experiences as children. We become less flexible, more dogmatic and fixed in our "habits" as we get older; but, the poem says, however the tracks of our lives diverge (and cross) from those of our contemporaries, we will share the experience of death, whether it takes us young (Dockery), or, at the end of the poem, as the "end of age".

The poem contains a series of five questions about Dockery, which cannot be answered, because he is dead; and then the question that shapes the poem- how do we come by the values which determine how we live our own life?

The locked door of the room the narrator occupied as a student symbolises the parts of human experience which he is now excluded from- specifically, having a family and owning a house. The thinking aloud in stanza 5 repeats this concept, in line 38. The thesis or argument is contained in the long speculative sentence which runs from line 38 to line 44.

To paraphrase it; something must determine whether we see ourselves as wanting to have children or not, and it is less a question of our fundamental values than a hardening of habit of the repetition of our way of life, day after day, into what comes to seem "quite natural" to us, even when it diverges from what other people do. We reach a point where "suddenly" those choices, which in theory we could change, become fixed ("all we've got", line 40).

In case this seems unconvincing, Larkin makes the language in the final stanza more definite, and less like a speculative, provisional train of thought. When you look back at your life hitherto, from the point at which these familiar habits have locked the door tight-shut to changes, you can see that this was your destiny from the beginning.

Lines 24 – 26 introduce the ways in which the lines or paths of our lives diverge or part, as the narrator's lack of commitments and attachments contrasts with Dockery's having a son at the age of nineteen or twenty, and the apparent confidence with which he saw the path of his future stretching before him. Those lines join again in the final four lines of the poem, where the underlying, universal shared experience in the lives of everyone is summed up as the sequence of boredom, fear (of death), and ultimately death itself.

The shortness of Dockery's life is not dwelled on or regretted (he must have died at the age of about 37-40). There is no sense of mourning or grief. The only "shock" lies in the narrator's realisation that other people of the same background and age as him have such different or divergent lives, and that he may no longer have the opportunities he thinks he has, as change is now, suddenly, impossible for him because he has become enslaved by his habits.

"How much had gone of life" (line 28) refers less to the deadline of death (as the poem is voiced by a man aged about 40) than to the deadening narrowing of his options.

The poem moves from "much" to "little" in line 19, and then to "no…..no…..no……no" (lines 25-26 and 32), "not" in line 36, and "nothing" in lines 43 and 44. This mirrors the process by which the poem limits and then destroys the possibility of personal change, and it accounts for the power of the simple inaccessibility of what lies behind a locked or shut door.

Ellipsis does not feature naturally in the work of a poet as preoccupied with rhyme and rhythm as Larkin- usually, everything is in its place. The ellipsis in line 19 and in line 32 creates the illusion of thinking aloud, but our narrator is bored, yawns and falls asleep. The blankness and the inevitability of death in the final line enables the poem to encapsulate the connection and sequence of "boredom, then fear"- it enacts it, from stanzas 3-6.

The poem is mainly in iambic pentameters, with slight variation (lines 1, 9, 20, 34, 37, 40, 45, 46). The most arresting of these exceptions to the rule is lines 45-46; as they are consecutive, the slight shortening of the line here highlights the key aphorism of the poem; these two lines read as a reflective epitaph on the lives of all of us. Strikingly, they do not say that, because death is random, and imminent for some of us, we should "seize the day" (carpe diem), like Larkin's seventeenth-century Hull predecessor, Marvell, in "To His Coy Mistress". There is no duty to "use" life, because, in the end, death is universal.

The poem meditates on the perspective death gives to our life- not to the unfortunate Dockery's. The lexis of death is embroidered into the poem all the way through- death-suited/ used to live/ ignored/ subside from view/ killed/ fell asleep/ furnace/ end/ parting/ gone…life/ nothing/ leaves/ end of age.

The rhyme scheme sets off, in the first stanza, as ABABCDCD; stanza 2 is ABABCDDC; stanza 3, ABBACDCD; stanza 4, ABCADCBD; stanzas 5 and 6, ABBCADDC. This pattern reflects the totality of the poem, too- if the rhyme schemes are our lives, they diverge or part in the first four stanzas, with their slight variations. Then, the identical two closing stanzas join the various patterns in the shutting and locking of the door of death and inaccessibility. The form and structure of the poem reinforce its central statement, that what differentiates our lives from other people's makes no difference when we all die.

We can "get" (beget) children, but what we get in our lives is "innate" or pre-destined. The tracks or lines of our lives may differ, but the boredom and fear we experience is the same as everyone else's. Our lives "reflect a strong / Unhindered moon"; this moon is realistic, not idealistic or romantic, and so is the poem. Rather as in "Nothing To Be Said", we can work, reproduce, have leisure time, and be alive in prehistoric cave-dwelling times or modern ones, but, in the end, each day is a day nearer to our own death.

Ignorance

Many of Larkin's poems are preoccupied with the idea that knowledge is provisional because truth is subjective. The last line of "Self's The Man"; the impossibility of really knowing other people ("Talking in Bed") or how they live ("The Large Cool Store"); the conditionality of the scepticism in "Church Going"; all of these point to the frustrating uncertainty with which Larkin perceives what he perceives. Even the stripping of emotion out of poetry- the focus on adopting a rational view from a position of detachment- leaves the concept of "truth" elusive. The distinction between what is true and what is not motivates his poems about advertising ("Essential Beauty"), and the issue of truth surfaces in "Talking in Bed", "Send No Money", the final stanza of "An Arundel Tomb".

The second stanza personifies "things", to which it ascribes flexible survival skills and a sense of identity; in the context of a poem which uses "strange" in lines 1, 6 and 10, perhaps it is not so strange to treat humanity here as though people were "things". The idea may be that if we do not understand psychology, we may as well be commenting on the behaviour of inanimate objects.

There is a contrast between knowing "nothing" in line 1 and wearing knowledge in line 11. The third stanza offers the thesis that we choose to have around us, in our personal space, what we know (it is familiar). There would be some logic and comfort in staying in these familiar surroundings, where we are unlikely to be worried by imponderable questions. Having studiously avoided the personal pronoun in the narrator's voice, the poem then uses the royal "we" and "our" from line 11 onwards. I take this plural to mean people like the poet/narrator- people whose vocation it is to find explanations for the perceived strangeness and the deficit in understanding our world, which we are all liable to feel.

The closing three lines point out that it is indeed "strange" (because there are no defining answers) to spend "all our life" investigating the strangeness of the human condition, when the consequence of doing so is that we still have no insight at the end of our own lives.

It is not a coincidence that this poem comes immediately after "Dockery and Son", which led us to the conclusion that one way of life (family, children) is no better or worse than another (being formally uncommitted, and childless).

The poem is called "Ignorance" because it argues that we know nothing, or next to nothing, about our universe- not scientifically, but philosophically or existentially. Nor are we likely to. However, the narrator does not intend to retire from the futile quest "to be sure".

It is the third- and last- of the thirty-two poems to have three-line stanzas, and the only one with this rhyme scheme of ABBCC.

It is idiosyncratic to give a poem the title "Ignorance"; we might expect one called "Knowledge" instead, but if knowledge or truth is beyond our grasp, we may as well concentrate on ignorance, on what we do not know, because at least we understand *that*.

Ignorance is something we should not celebrate; and, if you look through the titles of all the poems, you will find that none of them is celebratory. Larkin's is the poetry of observation and deduction- of what he terms "dilution" in "Dockery and Son"- rather than of celebration and exuberant spontaneity.

Reference Back

This poem has three stanzas of uneven lengths- 6, 9 and 7 lines. Each stanza ends with a full stop, but the rhyme scheme (AABBCC; AABBCCDDE; ABBCCDD) suggests that line 15 belongs in the final stanza. The rhymes become weaker and more tenuous as the poem develops; a brittle cheerfulness impels the verse, but it barely holds together in the final stanza.

The occasion appears to be a visit by Larkin to his mother, in 1953, when he is 30 or 31. His father had died three years earlier and his mother would now be 67. Larkin was working in Belfast and was involved with both Patsy Strang and Winifred Arnott. The most striking aspect of the poem is its use of the word "unsatisfactory"- not a poetic word- four times, to describe the hall, the room, his mother's age and his "prime"- the point in his life where he expects to be most alive.

In fact, the psychological process of decline, inertia (boredom?) and slow dying seems to have started already. His mother's pleasantly positive comment goes unanswered by a narrator who is preoccupied with his sense that his first thirty years of life have been wasted ("Dockery and Son" has already raised this topic, and "Send No Money" will do more with it).

The conceit in the poem is that his mother's remark will from now on spring to mind every time he plays the record, and so remind him that both he and his mother are dissatisfied. Moreover, the date of the recording- 1923- will remind Larkin of his own being an infant.

The nature of his mother's dissatisfaction, in particular, is not explained; he is only interested in his own perception of the recording (made thirty years earlier). It has not changed (although tastes in jazz had changed and become more modern in the meantime); by contrast, he sees his childhood, and human beings see their past, as a measurement of what they have lost- this presumably includes freshness and unfamiliarity, which yields to knowledge, as for the lambs in "First Sight"- if indeed we or they know anything- we might rather not have.

Bearing in mind that "knowledge" is presented as an illusion in the poem immediately prior to this one, we are faced here with "perspectives", or perceptions. This narrator perceives not just "losses" (of one parent? of innocence/ of enthusiasm?) but also an inkling that somehow we are responsible for those losses- a perception which cannot be grounded in fact.

As a pair of poems, this and "Ignorance" touch on the issues raised by existentialism. The existentialists would argue that because bad things happen to us randomly, not as a punishment for our own sins, we should try to disregard them, or at least not blame ourselves. Moreover, if we cannot determine our own success (Dockery made some calculated decisions, but his life did not turn out as he anticipated), what we do with our time and our lives- waste it, or use it- is of no consequence.

If virtue has no reward, then the social constraints of home, family, politeness, garden parties are irrelevant and there is no shame in fantasising, in sly admiration of wild or thuggish behaviour, or in idleness- all of which are presented in this collection without criticism. This set of poems, as a collection, shows us people- and animals- whose lives are meaningless (most of the men, women and children in the poems are not named or individualised), and people who think that their own lives are meaningless (his narrators). There is the occasional intervention of those who think their lives have some significance ("Naturally the Foundation Will Bear Your Expenses"), or who think they have found some personal significance (Dockery, Arnold, the faith healer, the pet-seeking children, the young mothers in "Afternoons") but all of them are wrong.

The sense of loss and decline- of confidence eroding- for the generation before Larkin's own (his mother's), is very clear in "Love Songs in Age", where the written songs are simply a tearful reminder of what has gone- freshness and brilliance, and the "unfailing sense of being young". It seems that that youthful enthusiasm can wane by our early thirties!

"Reference Back" puts flesh on the bones of the apparent truth of "Dockery and Son"- that life is boredom, then fear, as life "goes". The boredom is genuine during this dutiful visit to his mother, and the sense of lapsing into further losses, with the fear that accompanies it, shapes this poem, as it had "Next, Please" and will, again, more dramatically, in the final stanza of "Send No Money".

Larkin and his mother are in separate rooms in her house, but they hear the same record. Their lives are like the tracks of the railway, intersecting and diverging again; both are "unsatisfactory", and defined by what they have lost- a father or a husband. The poem presents the thesis that, whether you are in your sixties or your early thirties, your experience is equally "unsatisfactory", because people whose loss you feel (in the case of Sydney Larkin, the nature and keenness of this loss is a separate issue) are disappearing from your life.

Wild Oats

This is another semi- autobiographical and confessional poem, in which the narrator holds up for our inspection his incompetence at romantic relationships and at being confronted with his idealised version of beauty in physical form.

Although he says that it was (twenty years ago; not necessarily now) the beauty of a face which reduced him to helplessness, what he responds to in "bosomy rose" is not the Englishness, not the fur gloves, and not the rose; which leaves only the "bosomy" part! (we are reminded again of the "golden tits" in "Next, Please").

Line 4 reveals, sidelong, that he could not bring himself to speak to her, and so was left "to talk to….her friend in specs"- the less physically attractive "girl".

The narrator externalises his feelings about his own social inadequacy and lack of confidence by offering the perception that when he met "beautiful", she found him amusing or pathetic or both. Eleven of the poem's twenty-four lines are about her. She was, perhaps, the third person in his relationship- such as it was- with the second girl, "the friend". That relationship is dominated by statistics (seven years……over four hundred letters etc) because some things can be measured, but a blinding attraction cannot.

After the disclosures which reveal the narrator's defects comes the end of his relationship, in lines 17-21. The charge list is quite specific and comprises a list of three criticisms (too selfish, withdrawn/ And easily bored); the "agreement" is one in which he is passive, because it has not motivated him to adapt (line 21); that line is like swallowing medicine, grimly accepting, while disagreeing, under your breath, with the diagnosis which prescribes it. It is here that we feel least unsympathetic towards the narrator; however, he goes on to inform the reader that he has kept two photos of the beautiful girl in his wallet for twenty years- although she has had no place in his life. He is, if we are being generous to him, and accept his weakness for a pretty face, less a stalker than a harmless fantasist; but his acute maladjustment is apparent.

The poem is a dramatic monologue, and, in that tradition, it reveals- accidentally- aspects of the narrator's character which are not flattering to him. A man who counts his letters, goes to the trouble of recovering the engagement ring he gave, and undergoes five rehearsals (whether for the wedding service or the break-up is insouciantly left to us to imagine!), dismisses the end of his best prospect of marriage without much reflection or humility, and promptly returns to his obsession with the unattainable beauty of the other, with the uniquely attractive face, is a man who appears incapable of a normal emotional focus.

Line 14 is intriguing; what is meant by cathedral cities "unknown to the clergy"? During Larkin's lifetime there were 44 such cities in England; but the cathedral cities in which he met the "friend in specs" were perhaps not official cathedral cities at all, but sacred places (to him) unblessed by the Church and unconsecrated by the marriage he did not have; hotel rooms, perhaps.

When we relate this poem (written in 1962) to Larkin's life, the girl he was closest to marrying had been Ruth Bowman (who did wear glasses, and to whom Larkin had proposed, in 1948, having met her in 1944, when she was 16 and he was 22; he later explained this uncharacteristic gesture as a way of addressing his feeling that his isolationism was harmful- to him), and the beautiful one was Jane Exall, whom he met in 1946. Ruth broke their engagement off in 1950 when Larkin secured his professional move to Belfast.

The narrator is criticised as "withdrawn" and the thesis of the poem is half-hidden. The narrator seems to feel that his drive or attraction to women he finds physically beautiful is, to them, a matter of derision, and that this unsatisfactory instinct casts a blight over his relationships with the less attractive, who are interested in him until they find out how difficult he is to deal with, and how incapable he is of either being in love, as most people would judge it, or of being loved.

If he has in fact learnt anything, it is that he faces a life of dull solitude, and very little more than that. The phrase "easily bored" reminds us of the boredom, then fear, of "Dockery and Son"- a poem which similarly features calculations, numbers, and the isolation of the narrator, who faces the prospect of being alone for the rest of his life.

The cheery rhyme scheme at the end of the third stanza is a flourish; the rhyme of snaps/perhaps changes the rhyme scheme, which was ABCABDEF in the previous stanzas and now achieves a kind of ironic resistance, when the narrator's back is against the wall- ABCABDED.

Three-stanza poems with eight lines per stanza, elsewhere in this collection, are "Sunny Prestatyn" (which also, incidentally, mentions "huge tits"), "Love Songs in Age", "Naturally the Foundation will Bear Your Expenses", "Send No Money" and "Afternoons". All of these poems express dissatisfaction, more or less obliquely, and they become progressively darker in character. The "Sunny Prestatyn" connection is arguably the most significant, because both poems dramatise male discomfort with the ideal woman- a metaphor, perhaps, for the larger preoccupation of the collection as a whole with the unrealised and unrealisable dream.

Through Bleaney, Arnold and a host of narrative personae, Larkin repeatedly shows us the process of people settling for less than we (or they) could or should- because of our social difficulties and character defects, including chronic shyness and a politeness which inhibits us from expressing our real dreams and desires. Much of life, in these poems, is a quest to avoid, or accept, solitude or loneliness- a sense of missing out. That quest, however, is irrelevant in the context of our slow dying; whatever epoch we live in, and however we are able to spend our days, we all die, and, in that sense, there is "Nothing To Be Said".

Essential Beauty

A poem which at first appears to be in an observational style- listing the many advertising images visible on the "rained-on streets and squares" of Hull (not Prestatyn!)- turns darker at line 24. Until this point, we have read images of eight different product campaigns- for bread, custard, motor oil, salmon, butter, milk, oxo cubes (?), hot bedtime drinks. Then, as stanza two opens, we are exposed to the aspirational language of advertising- pure/ new/ clean- which exhorts us to buy products and then "rise/ serenely" into a better life.

The verbs in the opening stanza (screen, cover, shine) suggest a process of artistic or aesthetic creativity, rather like a commercial photographer's. As the advertising images accumulate, they are developed in greater detail, with the illusion of homeliness occupying three whole lines (12-15).

The contrast in lines 22-23 between dark and white leads to a triptych of the deceived; a boy who is violently sick after drinking beer or some other alcoholic drink; a pensioner who paid extra for a brand of tea which promised a longer life-span; and, specifically, the "dying smoker" who faces a disturbing, personified image of death. These are the images the billboards choose not to exhibit – that alcohol, nicotine (neither of which Larkin resisted) and other substances can harm us and abbreviate our lives. Larkin himself would die prematurely from the spread of oesophageal cancer.

The structure of the poem- which takes us from apparently innocent advertising posters to death- contrasts the visible and tangible- the products- with the intangible, the feelings ownership is intended to induce, and the desire to have the life the posters promise, because it seems to be one where we will feel safe and our senses are heightened or more intense.

Our "eyes/ That stare beyond this world" compare the imperfections in our own lives with the (repeated) purity and elevated (literally, on the billboards, and aspirationally) experience implied by the advertisements. The poem is adorned with the language of ancient and more modern religions, and with rituals of cleansing- groves, how life should be, high above, each hand stretches towards, cups, rise, proclaim, pure, beyond this world, new, washed quite clean, home, white-clothed, water.

In the closing lines, it is reality, as opposed to imagination, which prevails; instead of the smiles of the well-balanced family, in the light outdoors, we have the smile of death, and eyes which go dark as they see "beyond this world".

The relentlessness of death in the closing lines is remarkable; death will not be kept at a distance by the exhaling of cigarette smoke, or be kept away in the dark by the lighting up of a smoker's match. A similar tone of helplessness in the face of our own destiny also informs "Ambulances". The poems in the second half of the collection are much darker, cumulatively, than the first half; the immutable fact of our death, the failure of interpersonal relationships, and the gap between what we wish for and what we have are the three themes which dominate the final eight poems, from "Dockery and Son" on.

Send No Money

Here is another poem in three stanzas, and in stanzas of eight lines- the form which Larkin seems most comfortable with. As we would expect, the final stanza includes a striking image- of "the bestial visor"- and an attempt at something sententious, overegged by alliteration, which remains rather unconvincing because it is obscure.

"Wild Oats" has exactly the same form, and it, too, contrasts the unsatisfactory present with the unsatisfactory past. In tone, though, "Send No Money" is closer to "A Study of Reading Habits", in its recording of unresolved frustration and unanswered questions.

Our narrator this time wants, as a boy, to know "the truth", and find out how the world works- what its guiding principles are. Satisfied that he has no ulterior motive, Time tells him to observe patiently: it is by watching, rather than being involved unthinkingly in the world (having "a bash") that the narrator can develop the detachment which promises some kind of insight, although we have seen, in "Ignorance", how partial and incomplete that is.

The boy, who speaks in monosyllables, seems undeveloped and unquestioning; he is in the company of "the other lads there" and seems to be an adolescent.

The first two stanzas are separated from the third by half a lifetime; half of Larkin's lifetime would have taken him to the age of 31, or to 1953. In his earlier poem "I Remember, I Remember", Larkin had written about his childhood as a series of non-events; it was utterly unremarkable, and nothing significant happened during it. Here, he describes his "youth" as spent "tracing….truth", but, evidently, not finding it.

Is this detachment from an orthodox engagement with people, hobbies, interests, aims, dreams- this preoccupation with "the long perspectives" of mortality and loss- a sacrifice worth making? Larkin presents it not as a sacrifice, but as a matter of fact- there is, in effect, no choice between being a doer or a watcher- at least for him, the watching is the only mode he can cope with.

That is not to say that the frustration of finding how elusive "truth" is- so that whatever we can say, as poets or truth-tellers, is provisional, speculative, tentative (especially in "Ignorance") - is without pain. After all, "Half life is over now", and, in stanza 3, the narrator sees, "full face on…….the bestial visor…….bent in by the blows" of the random acts of violence which "clobber life out" of us, whatever our protective armour. This poem is therefore an artistic manifesto; it makes the point that, however dedicated and detached the poet manages to be, any insight or truth into the human condition is "never sure", to quote "Ignorance" again. These two poems need to be read together. In "Ignorance" there is a sense, in stanza 2, that we can see that the world we live in is flexible and mutable, so that it must be governed by a principle of evolution; but, the poem tells us, our thinking is not so flexible or holistic, so we remain outsiders in the world we occupy, incapable of discerning the truth which governs it.

In "Send No Money", half a life of seeking truth, by watching, has led nowhere- to "Sod all"; the only apparent principle is that life is completely random. The alliteration of "t" in the final two lines of the poem implies frustration; the pursuit of truth is futile, because it is unreachable, and chasing it is like wearing a straitjacket ("truss")- a confining garment from which it is difficult to escape.

Why would we send (no) money? We send money to disaster appeals, to rescue the innocent victims. Here, though, we have an instruction to send NO money- the impoverished casualty of waiting for truth does not need, or deserve, external support, financial or otherwise.

As a mail-order advertising technique, too, it used to be common to buy goods on approval, which involved the instruction to send no money up front. The title of the poem is not anything Time says to the narrator. It is, rather, an instruction from the narrator to the reader- don't get your hopes up that you can buy in advance some knowledge of how life on earth operates, because all we can say is that what happens to us "happened to happen"- it is random. As the closing line of "Reference Back" concludes, the process of watching our life shrink and deteriorate is something we cannot influence.

The use of alliteration and rhyme is sardonic, but it militates against self-pity. The narrator here has taken up a position as an adolescent observer of the accidental or random damage time does to people's lives, keenly and with gratitude (line 15), and he expects to need patience.

The poem is an ironic and somewhat desperate complaint or protest about how long it has taken not to establish truth- and about the probable continuing failure of such a mission- but it does not lay its tools down, or refuse to continue; this may be a random choice, but it is a choice, and choices cannot, once made, be unmade, in the world of these poems.

Afternoons

With its falling autumn leaves (in ones or twos, single (children's) lives and couples' lives) this poem is an epitaph for those who are still very much alive- young parents. It adopts an anti-marriage and anti-children stance, suggesting that retaining the beauty in our lives and the sense of having our own aims and priorities is incompatible with either; remember that the value of Dockery's parenthood and Arnold's marriage have both been questioned, because of the loss of selfhood these human connections necessarily involve. Sharing your life with others dilutes or diminishes it.

It is only recently that the "young mothers" who are the subject of the poem acquired restrictive responsibilities- not long ago, they were lovers with courting- places and romantic dreams. After marrying, those dreams are nailed into a wedding photo album, forming an inert record of the past, which lies "near the television" and its moving pictures. Romance (and unmarried sex) has been replaced with "estatefuls of washing", and their husbands are behind them, while their children's expectations and demands are before them- their priorities have been re-ordered, and they themselves are squeezed, sideways.

In this poem, the language of pre-married love coexists with, and is suppressed by, the childish language of infancy, school and play. Lives which are themselves "unripe acorns" are being pushed out by the "pushing" of childbirth, prams and pushchairs. Being pushed to the side of your own life is a hollowing out, and a matter of elegiac sadness (fading/ fall/ lying); it is as though the young mothers have transferred their own potential to their children, while they should still be growing, themselves; parents too young, they will never reach the maturity, the sense of selfhood, which enables us to shape our own lives, and their "beauty" is already being transmuted into something thick, static, different and much less attractive.

The vagueness and lack of purpose in their lives now is matched in the rhyme scheme, which is almost non-existent, with only the echo of "-ing" (lines 1,3, 11, 13) and the poignant repetition of "courting-places" – which itself implies that this is a repetitive cycle, like the weddings and the washing; becoming a parent at a young age means giving up your ability to shape your own life. Setting your children free means marginalising yourself and any lingering dreams of romance; the wedding album is an artefact, and the drudgery of men's work and women's washing ensures that it is of historic interest. It will not take decades for these wedding albums to become redundant, like the sheet music in "Love Songs in Age". These mothers will be like the women in "Faith Healing", with unfulfilled dreams of what their lost potential could have motivated them to do.

Many of the poems in this collection have concentrated on the unfulfilled potential in older lives, but this one reminds us that younger lives can be unfulfilled too, and not necessarily through the solitude and detachment of the poet/ narrator. Parenthood was bad for Dockery, for Arnold, and it will be, too, for these young mothers, and the anonymised fathers who stand behind them.

An Arundel Tomb

The final poem in "The Whitsun Weddings" can be expected to bring together and summarise some of the key themes and concepts. At 42 lines (seven stanzas of six lines), it is the third longest of the 32 poems.

The tomb is that of Richard Fitzalan, 10th Earl of Arundel, (born in 1306 or 1313) and his second wife, Eleanor of Lancaster (born in 1318); they died in 1376 and 1372 respectively. The memorial is in Chichester Cathedral; however, the Earl is buried in Lewes Priory. He was first married to a nine-year-old girl, Isabel le Dispenser, when he was either eight or fifteen; the Pope annulled that marriage in 1344. He married Eleanor in 1345. She was a widow, and the first cousin of his first wife. The content of the Earl's Will suggests that the affection which the effigy depicts was real.

Larkin spoke of how he was struck by the "affecting" pose of the effigy. In "MCMX1V", Larkin had presented the post-First World War world as one which had lost its "innocence"; this coincides with the rise of modernism as a literary genre, with its sense of self-absorption and its critique and exploration of a general loss of a sense of purpose or direction.

Now, Larkin goes back to the 14th century and contemplates what this dead couple "would not think.....would not guess". He surmises that the attitude of love which the sculptor chose to depict was not intended to be a public statement, centuries later; it was just a spontaneous, "thrown off" gesture, which they "hardly meant". The memorial is unchangeable- "in stone"; so this accidental detail has become a misrepresentation, because the sculpture continues to be seen or read by successive generations as an emblem of the romantic, rather than as a memorial of a particular couple. Romanticising love in a memorial about death, or symbolising an idealised married love in a memorial which has lasted for centuries, is not, according to Larkin, the purpose of art or poetry.

After the musings on the inaccessibility of truth, and the impersonality of time, in the last few poems, Larkin picks on the effigy as a lie (lines 2,13) and says that Time has turned it into "Untruth". The alliteration of "t" here reminds us of the last lines of "Send No Money", where time simply hammers the life out of the individual, through a series of random "occurrence"(s). The closing lines of "An Arundel Tomb" muse on "our almost-instinct" that something of us survives death- a romanticised fantasy, as if wishing it to be true could make it true. It is, though, *not quite an instinct* (because there is no evidence to support its truth) and it is *not quite true*; in fact, nothing survives of us in the "bone-riddled ground".

The poem is in two distinct sections; the first three stanzas depict the effigy, but half way through the fourth stanza the focus shifts away from the couple to the people who visit the Cathedral through an endless succession of the passing centuries.

Stanzas 5 and 6, particularly 6, are puzzling, because of the language; why the smoke? "Trough" and "hollow" introduce the concept of emptiness, and refer to the "hollows of afternoons" in the previous poem. Stanza 5 seems obscure. It may perhaps contain a historical allusion. In 1377, a poll tax of four pence per adult was introduced, to finance a new army to attack France; shortly afterwards, in June 1377, Edward 3rd died, and a period of military frustration ensued ("soundless damage"?). The "old tenantry" may refer to the previous system of taxation, where the lord of the manor decided each family's tax liability.

The couple's oxymoronic "stationary journey" through the time after their own lifetimes sees a succession of "endless altered people" who come "washing at their identity"- a pun on the washing in "Afternoons" and the water in "Water". Why do people continue to visit the effigy in the Cathedral? Presumably, to try to find a connection with the past, the "long perspectives" of "Reference Back"- but one of the conclusions these poems draw is that the past means nothing ("sod all"). Larkin had no time for sentiments such as the notion that love is stronger than death.

The narrator's certainty that nothing of us survives our existential dissatisfaction, and his detached scepticism about time and about the misrepresentation of the content of life (when we indulge romanticised thinking), distance the reader from him; we would like to believe that the final line of this final poem can be believed in, without irony, but to do this would be to misread the rest of the poem which precedes it- just as to romanticise the hand-holding on the effigy would be to misread the memorial.

The concept of misrepresenting the truth, through or over time, extends to the effigy itself. Judging from the images I have seen, lines 9-12 are inaccurate- although the couple hold hands, his left hand and lower arm are missing from the stone memorial in its present form. However, Larkin was able to investigate the effigy's history and made notes on this- perhaps including notes about its earlier condition and design, before the left arm was damaged or vandalised.

It is characteristic of Larkin that he should throw the reader a sentimental crumb of comfort at the very end of the collection, as if he challenges us to pick it up. We should not be tempted to do so.

Just as "Granny Graveclothes' Tea" promised to ward off death, falsely, and just as smokers think until the very last moment that their smoking is not really bringing death nearer (in "Essential Beauty"), the idea that there is an emotional part "of us" which survives us is, for Larkin, an evident untruth.

Perhaps he would direct us, at the end of our reading, our journey through the poems, to the opening one, "Here", and to its last three lines, in which there is a sudden end of solid land; beyond it is "unfenced" air, and all of us will disappear into it when the ambulance comes for us.

Appendix 1- Larkin's themes, methods and interests

You will have noticed, as you read the poems, that Larkin believes that good poems are crafted, with careful attention to structure, form, rhyme and metre. Many of the poems in this collection were years in the writing. Occasionally, we may feel that a rhyme is forced, but we are rarely conscious that the rhyme scheme of a poem has dictated a particular choice of word.

Larkin evades or obscures the structural straitjacket of rhyme by adopting a flexible approach to the rhythm of his lines, their punctuation, the discursive vocabulary he uses, and the way he constructs his sentences. Sometimes this is unorthodox, either because he wants us to feel that the poem is excavating a buried nugget of gold, with difficulty, or because he wants to capture a sense of bewilderment, of being unable to get out of the maze of human experience and cosmic irrelevance. The very first sentence of "Here" runs to twenty-four and a half lines, and it describes "swerving" through a varied landscape to a solitary destination, which can be interpreted as either creativity, or death, or both.

He has a wide range of narrative voices. Sometimes the narrator is a sardonic or satirised version of himself. He finds it easier to tolerate hypocrisy in others than in himself, though he tends to forgive himself as well. Larkin's dislike of pretentiousness is clear from the people he chooses to write about (mostly ordinary, anonymous people leading dull or frustrated lives) and from the simple, demotic language which dominates. There is no room for the grandiloquent or rhetorical gesture; his interest is in wringing poetry- or poetic truth- from the everyday, the ordinary, the unexceptional, the merely workmanlike.

Larkin usually stands on the border of the scene his poems describe- he looks at the park, the playground, the street with the ambulance in it, the railway platforms, the Arundel Tomb, the advertising boards. He sits on the train with the Whitsun newly-weds but he does not talk with them; he takes Bleaney's room but he does not meet him; he visits his mother but does not converse with her; he lies in bed but gives nothing away. He sits under the belly of Time, and waits for revelations that never come. He takes out the plain girl but keeps the photos of "beautiful" in his wallet for twenty years.

The poems are personal and, up to a point, confessional; Larkin uses them to allude to his own tastes and eccentricities, without analysing them head-on. The experiences he uses as the foundations on which the finished poems are built include fictionalised Oxford contemporaries, anonymised female lovers (Monica Jones, Maeve Brennan, Ruth Bowman), his own mother and his library colleague Arthur Wood. The finished poems are, however, never merely autobiographical. There is always an attempt- however frustrated or partially successful- to go from the particular, in his own life, to the general- to something readers recognise as relevant to them too. The popularity of this collection, and the recognition Larkin was given in his own lifetime, proves that he largely succeeded in this.

English culture and society are very different now from how they were fifty years ago. Hull was an expanding city, rather like the "New Towns" which followed in the next twenty years. Its development ushered in new shops, a new attitude to consumerism and advertising, and an ongoing failure to empower the majority through better education. We are less class-conscious now, but we still have an underclass whose prospects in life are limited by a lack of skills.

These people still populate the superstore, the park, the playground, the factory, the cemetery, and their own bedrooms and kitchens, with the same lack of drive that these poems chronicle. That much is timeless. The social disaffection which, more recently, has led to riots, terrorism and anti-social behaviour is absent from the quietly obedient and conformist blue- and white-collar world of Larkin's 1950s, just as a more proactive form of feminism is as far beyond the scope of the poster- girl in Prestatyn as it is beyond the imagination of the 14th century Eleanor Fitzalan.

Larkin's own temperament, and the internal conflicts he could not resolve in his own personal life, leak into the poems. Marry or stay single? Be a parent? Revere women, or objectify them- or both? Commit to one woman, or "think of the others" you could still meet? Live after the First World War/ the Industrial Revolution/the Neanderthal era? In the town or on the coast? In England or Northern Ireland? Become your habits or resist the hardening of habit into a life choice?

We could construct a long and detailed list. The main preoccupations are these- less importantly, how do men find a way of dealing with women which enriches them both (as women are "natureless in ecstasies", prone to "re-awake at kindness", and "too good for this life")? And, more importantly, how do we all- men and women- find meaning in our lives, when, lying ahead of us, there is only "age, and then the only end of age….recognising, and going dark"?

Your reading will reveal other recurring themes, such as existential angst, the fundamental dishonesty of advertising, a reaction against modernism, how our personality is formed……….. make your own list, and prioritise it, bearing in mind how much relative prominence the poems give to each idea.

While, for A-level students, there may be little time for deep research into the social context from which these poems emerged, any time you spend reading about the culture of England between 1945 and 1965, and Larkin's own biography, will help your understanding considerably. You should also be aware that a better understanding of the contexts in which the texts were produced, and are now received and judged, will lead you to a higher mark and a higher grade in your exam.

Appendix 2: the essays

Here are two sample essays, designed to offer you a sense of how an analysis of a poem can look for an A-level essay, with the required focus on form, structure and language.

Sample essay 1

Explore how Larkin presents his experience of reading in "A Study of Reading Habits"

Larkin uses short lines of 6-8 syllables, and a simple rhyme scheme ABCBAC, over three stanzas, to convey a sense of energy and frustration, which goes nowhere and leaves him disillusioned. His narrator analyses his experience of reading as so unsatisfactory that he now prefers drinking to reading ("Get stewed").

In each stanza, the language he adopts reflects the low tone of the material he has read- first, superhero or cartoon fantasy (lines 4-6), then horror and science fiction (8-12), and finally the Western pulp fiction (17-20). Although he has read extensively in the field of action and fantasy violence (including violence towards women), he has not found an authentic voice of his own. Reading to escape (a dull life) is an ineffectual substitute for making friends in the real world.

The poem is a dramatic monologue, so the interest lies in the persona of the narrator, and in what he accidentally reveals about himself. It is an issue of social maladjustment. The opening stanza hints at an unhappy childhood, especially at school, where the narrator may have been bullied because he was short-sighted. The violent self-defence he would have liked to deliver to bigger boys stayed between the pages of the books he read.

Stanza 2 goes on, chronologically, to teenage or young adult years. The narrator fantasises about overpowering women sexually, but there is no sense that he has any skills in dealing with them, or that he would even have known what to do with a woman! The violence here is comical, because it is ironic or unreal, but the syntax in lines 9-10 is ugly, dysfunctional, and it puts "me" first. Only the most passive of women would find Dracula seductive; "clubbed" is a primitive verb, and it lacks all subtlety.

The rhyme of fangs/ meringues makes the violence seem harmless, because it requires no effort to break up a meringue. However, the impression remains that the narrator was – and maybe still is- incapable of relating to the opposite sex or forming friendships- a continuation of the social ineptitude hinted at in the opening stanza and his primary school years.

In stanza 3, he concedes that he identifies with cowards, who stand on the edge of the action, looking on, rather than with the hero who gets the girl; in fact, he "lets the girl down" and loses her to the hero. His sense of his own inadequacy has grown stronger, the more he has read, and the gap between what he would like to be and what he is is so large that he can no longer bear to "read much now". Ending the poem with a slang expletive is a final outburst of (sexual) frustration.

The poem is notable for its reliance on very simple language and especially on monosyllabic words There is nothing poetic or elevated in the language or the tone; adjectives seem incidental and slight, and a dark, brooding dissatisfaction dominates the poem. The ellipsis in line 17, omitting the personal pronoun "I", implies that the narrator has become less comfortable with his own identity, as his reading and his capacity for relationships has continued to misfire.

Beneath its grim humour, the poem hints at some kind of truth; that if we think we can model ourselves on the heroes of low fiction, we are wrong. The thought that we could reveals more about our own inadequacies than about the value of reading. This narrator reads not to learn or to be entertained but to escape into a series of parallel worlds (cartoons, horror, the western) in genres where life is artificially simple- a reflection of his own naivete and limitations. Our choices in what we read can therefore teach us something, or teach us nothing; perhaps we can tell a person's personality from the newspaper they read or the books they have in their homes.

(645 words)

Sample essay 2

Explore how Larkin explores his experience of attachment in "Wild Oats".

This poem has its roots in Larkin's time in Belfast, and his relationships with the glamorous Jane Exall (an unrealised fantasy) and the less glamorous Ruth Bowman, to whom he was engaged, but never married; the poem was written thirteen years after the start of the narrative it relates.

The poem addresses, honestly and with comic frankness, the narrator's inability to deal with beauty, as he perceives it. The "bosomy English rose" with the unique face (perhaps an allusion to the face of Helen of Troy in Greek mythology, that "launched a thousand ships" and the Trojan War) is out of his league, and he knows it.

He feels defensive in her presence, and thinks she is laughing at him; but he makes sure that, after his engagement to her plain friend is over, the one thing he has kept (for twenty years, in his wallet) is two photos of her, which give him some erotic stimulation- and the last laugh. This is the triumph of the average, the disadvantaged- a version of Beauty and the Beast.

The literal quality of his actual relationship, with "the friend in specs", is underpinned by plain language, and peppered with the ordinary; who can be stimulated by statistics? He measures his (past) love in numbers, not adjectives; he makes sure he gets the engagement ring back, because it was a poor investment. The impact of the plain girl, over seven years, four hundred letters, and sex in many locations, still reverberates much less than the unattainable and irresistible power of "beautiful", whom he encountered only twice.

The third stanza shifts the focus from the girls to the narrator, and concedes (or does it?) that his ineptitude at intimate relationships with women is due to his own defects (lines 19-20). However, what he has "learnt" is not really absorbed; it is the judgment of the woman who eventually lost her patience with him. He is failing to acknowledge the reasons for his romantic failure. The comedy of this final stanza is acute; in the closing three lines, it emerges that, having failed to absorb the lesson from his real relationship, which would make it possible for him to do better in future, he clings instead to the idealised image of "bosomy rose". The definition of her in terms of two symbols, and his failure to give either woman (or "girl") a name, highlights the gap in the narrator's psyche between actual relationships with women and imaginary ones.

While the ten uses of the pronouns "I" and "me", in a poem only 24 lines long, emphasise the narrator's egomania- which could alienate the reader- the wry admission in the final line, that he knows that keeping the photographs does not bode well for his future dealings with real women, rehabilitates him somewhat.

In calling his former fiancee's damning judgement "an agreement", the narrator concedes that he is imperfect, and he avoids conflict, with the same evasion and lack of confidence which stopped him from speaking to "beautiful" in the first place.

The failure to engage with who (or what) you really want, because your self-esteem, or your skills, are (in your own view) inadequate, is something most of us will have experienced. This poem is a dramatic monologue, and the narrator's obsessive personality does him no credit. But the poem is both about him and about the reader- it asks us how sure we are that we are calling love love, and it challenges us to take the road less travelled- to engage with what will fire us with emotional intensity, rather than a dull compromise with the less beautiful.

(605 words)

Appendix 3

Key dates and events in Larkin's life

Born 9 August 1922

1943 graduated from St John's College Oxford with First Class degree in English Literature

November 1943   Appointed Librarian at the public library in Wellington, Shropshire

1944 Met 16-year-old Ruth Bowman; engaged 1948-50

1946 Met Monica Jones in Leicester; she eventually moved in with him in 1982, after a period in hospital.

October 1950 Appointed Sub-Librarian at Queen's University Belfast

March 1955 Became Librarian at the University of Hull. Met Maeve Brennan; their relationship began in 1960 and continued until 1978

October 1955 "The Less Deceived" published

1964   "The Whitsun Weddings" published

1965 Awarded Queen's Gold Medal for Poetry

1961-71 Wrote jazz reviews for the Daily Telegraph

1973 Edited The Oxford Book of Twentieth Century English Verse

1974 "High Windows" published

1975 Awarded CBE. Began relationship with his secretary Betty Mackereth

1984 Offered post of Poet Laureate; he declined it

1985 Awarded Companion of Honour. Health failed. Died of cancer on 2 December 1985 aged 63.

Appendix 4

Dates of individual poems and social history context

<u>Completion dates for the individual poems in "The Whitsun Weddings" are as follows-</u>

Here
8/10/61

Mr Bleaney
May 1955

Nothing to be Said
18/10/61

Love Songs in Age
1/1/57

Naturally the Foundation………
22/2/61

Broadcast
6/11/61

Faith Healing
10/5/60

For Sidney Bechet
15/1/54

Home is So Sad
31/12/58

Toads Revisited
Oct 1962

Water
6/4/54

The Whitsun Weddings
18/10/58

Self's the Man
5/5/58

Take One Home for the Kiddies
13/8/60

Days
3/8/53

MCMXIV
17/5/60

Talking in Bed
10/8/60

The Large Cool Store
18/6/61

A Study of Reading Habits
20/8/60

As Bad as a Mile
9/2/60

Ambulances
10/1/61

The Importance of Elsewhere
13/6/55

Sunny Prestatyn
Oct 1962

First Sight
3/3/56

Dockery and Son
28/3/63

Ignorance
11/9/55

Reference Back
21/8/55

Wild Oats
12/5/62

Essential Beauty
26/6/62

Send No Money
21/8/62

Afternoons
Sept 1959

An Arundel Tomb
20/2/56

The poems cover the period 1954-1963.

A passing knowledge of social history helps us to put how Larkin thought into context with what was going on around him in society.

- Food rationing after the Second World War ended in Britain in July 1954.

- In 1952, only 8% of homes had a television, and programmes were only transmitted for five hours per day.

- Shopping was done at the local corner shop, and major household items were bought using hire purchase (a very regulated type of credit); consumer debt was unimaginable.

- Women were still seen as primarily homemakers, but as living standards rose more women took paid jobs outside the home.

- In 1960 the average number of children per family was 2.6; it is now 1.74.

- In 1957, fridges were to be found in just 15% of homes; most people rented their home. In the same year, the average price of a house was £2,170. Men earned an average of £190 per annum in 1959.

- Only 30% of homes were owner-occupied, and the private rented housing in which almost half the population lived (like Mr Bleaney) was often cold and uncomfortable.

- Instead of the car boot sale, or trading on ebay, the rag and bone man, with his horse-drawn cart, would collect junk.

- The stereo LP first appeared in 1958. The Barbie doll was invented in 1959. Britain was a manufacturing country, producing steel, clothing, ships, aeroplanes and clothing.

- There was very little immigration; in 1951, less than 3% of the population of 50 million people had been born abroad, and only 140,000 BME citizens lived in Britain. Immigration arose mostly from the British Commonwealth and Central Europe. Starting with India and Pakistan in 1947, the British Empire was largely dismantled as more and more parts of it were granted independence by 1964.

- Most children left school at the age of 15, without qualifications. The university student was typically a privately educated middle-class male.

- Divorce, and having children outside of marriage, were less common. Homosexuality was a criminal offence. Prostitution was conducted openly, prior to the 1959 Street Offences Act.

- The era in which these poems were written was governed by the Conservatives (from 1951 to 1964); Churchill retired as Prime Minister at the age of 80 in 1955, and Sir Anthony Eden and Harold Macmillan succeeded him. Macmillan won the 1959 General Election on a mood of higher living standards ("you've never had it so good").

- Shops were closed on Sundays and there was no commercial sport on that day of the week. Half the population had an annual seaside holiday, often in a holiday camp. The post-war austerity with high rates of income tax gradually faded; the growth of service industries, technology and consumerism led to social change and a greater emphasis on novelty and youth.

- Commercial television began in 1955, and BBC 2 started in 1964. In 1957 Britain became a nuclear power- only the third, after the US and the USSR.

- The first motorway was built in 1958. A major expansion of universities (including Hull and its library) began in 1963. In 1964 the abolition of retail pricing laws encouraged the rise of supermarkets.

In October 1964 Harold Wilson became a Labour Prime Minister. This ushered in the abolition of the death penalty, and the start of comprehensive education, both in 1965.

When Larkin's letters were published posthumously, there was a critical backlash against his apparently misogynistic and racist views. However, even such a brief survey as this shows that social values were very different in the years 1955-1965 from the ones we are familiar with; racial segregation was only criminalised in the USA in 1964, and cheap international air travel was the invention of the 1960s.

We tend to underestimate the parochialism with which Britain faced the world at the time Larkin was writing these poems. He wrote just before sweeping changes, both in attitudes and 'everyday' living, would make Britain closer to how we are today.

 Gavin Smithers is a private tutor based in Chipping Campden, Gloucestershire. He has an English degree from Oxford University, and a passion for helping students to discover the joy and satisfaction of great literature.

So….if there's anything you're not sure about and your teacher can't help, please do contact the author- grnsmithers@hotmail.co.uk

Gavin's Guides are short books packed with insight. Their key aim is to help you raise your grade. For full details, look up Gavin's author page on Amazon.co.uk

Other titles include:

Understanding Arthur Miller's All My Sons. Understanding J.B. Priestley's An Inspector Calls. Understanding George Orwell's Animal Farm. Understanding William Golding's Lord of the Flies. Understanding Charles Dickens' Great Expectations. Understanding John Steinbeck's Of Mice and Men. Understanding Emily Dickinson's Set Poems. Understanding Edward Thomas' Set Poems. Understanding Harper Lee's To Kill A Mockingbird. Understanding Andrew Marvell's Cromwell & Eulogy Poems. Understanding Poems of the Decade for A level Edexdcel Poetry. Understanding Kazuo Ishiguro's Never Let Me Go. Understanding Jerusalem by Jez Butterworth

Printed in Great Britain
by Amazon